GIFTED
to SERVE

GIFTED to SERVE

T.L. LOWERY

Whitaker House

GIFTED TO SERVE

Dr. T. L. Lowery
Lowery Ministries International, Inc.
P.O. Box 2550
Cleveland, TN 37320

ISBN: 0-88368-525-6
Printed in the United States of America
Copyright © 1997 by Lowery Ministries International, Inc.

Whitaker House
30 Hunt Valley Circle
New Kensington, PA 15068

Library of Congress Cataloging-in-Publication Data

Lowery, T. L. (Thomas Lanier), 1929–
    Gifted to serve / T. L. Lowery.
        p.   cm.
    Includes bibliographical references.
    ISBN 0-88368-525-6 (alk. paper)
    1. Baptism in the Holy Spirit. 2. Gifts, Spiritual. I. Title.
BT123.L68 1998
234'.13—dc21   98–17070

1 2 3 4 5 6 7 8 9 10 11 12 / 08 07 06 05 04 03 02 01 00 99 98

ENDORSEMENTS

Few Christians these days are still debating whether all the New Testament spiritual gifts are valid and in use today. But what exactly are they? How can I discover and use my gifts? Dr. T. L. Lowery has provided us the dynamic guidebook that we need. When you read this book, you will have no doubt that you are *Gifted to Serve!*

C. PETER WAGNER
FULLER THEOLOGICAL SEMINARY

In his book *Gifted to Serve,* Dr. T. L. Lowery emphasizes the importance of having a strong foundation in the Lord. No matter how long you have been a Christian or where you are in your walk with Him, true holiness will only come as you walk in integrity and humility. Dr. Lowery has reminded us again that victory is not in methods, but in returning to the basics of knowing God through fasting, prayer, and the Word.

BENNY HINN
WORLD OUTREACH CENTER

Dr. T. L. Lowery has written one of the most profound books on the gifts of the Holy Spirit for this generation. In it he unveils how you can operate in the power of these gifts and how they will propel you into the presence of God. I believe that as you read this book, your relationship with God will be revolutionized, and you will never be the same again!

ROD PARSLEY
WORLD HARVEST CHURCH

I recommend *Gifted to Serve* for anyone who is interested in the gifts of the Spirit in our day. Although this book is well documented, it is also highly readable. It would make an excellent gift to a friend who wishes to learn more about the Holy Spirit.

DR. VINSON SYNAN
DEAN, SCHOOL OF DIVINITY, REGENT UNIVERSITY

In his book *Gifted to Serve,* Dr. T. L. Lowery presents both the biblical foundation and contemporary meaning of the gifts of the Spirit. In this day of stressful living and secular challenge of the Christian faith, these "enablements" of the Spirit are more important than ever. This is a book of relevant meaning for every person truly seeking to be led of the Spirit.

PAUL L. WALKER, PH.D.
GENERAL OVERSEER, CHURCH OF GOD

DEDICATION

I dedicate this book to the memory of my loving
parents who reared me in a godly environment.
Especially do I dedicate it to my wonderful daughter-
in-law Janice, and to my precious grandchildren
Aimee, Stephanie, John, and Michael,
whom I trust will carry on my vision.

CONTENTS

FOREWORD

I appreciate Dr. T. L. Lowery's straightforward approach to the gifts of the Spirit presented in this book. It is both a helpful biblical overview of the topic for new and searching believers, and a refreshing reminder for all Christians of the real purpose for the gifts. His timely emphasis is essential for the church today; spiritual gifts are not to be used to display our own "spirituality" or to call attention to ourselves, but to fulfill God's purposes and to extend His grace to the church and to the world.

The book includes a crucial chapter on the manifestation of spiritual gifts in church history. It shows how the Holy Spirit has been active throughout the centuries since the early church by providing historical references that reveal how God has continued to pour out His Spirit in every age: from the first centuries of the church through the Reformation, the Great Awakenings, the Holiness and Deeper Life movements, Pentecostalism, the interdenominational charismatic movement, and on to today. It addresses the objections of those who feel

9

that the gifts are no longer relevant for the church, and reminds Christians of all backgrounds of the continuity of the work of God through the Holy Spirit.

I have known Dr. Lowery for many years and appreciate him as a friend and for the powerful ministry God has given him. I pray that as you read his helpful and insightful book, you will ask God to use you to fulfill His purposes through your life, as you receive the love, power, and presence of God that He has provided through the precious gift of His Spirit.

"May the grace of the Lord Jesus Christ, and the love of God, and the fellowship of the Holy Spirit be with you all" (2 Corinthians 13:14).

ROBERT WHITAKER, SR.
WHITAKER HOUSE

PREFACE

THIS BOOK IS the result of a tremendous amount of study about the gifts of the Holy Spirit. It is my desire to place a book in your hands that will help you understand all aspects of a life empowered by the Spirit. On the pages that follow, you will find a reservoir of scriptural information to guide you in exploring various gifts of the Spirit that will enrich your walk with the Lord.

God desires every Christian to manifest His presence. This is a book you will want to share with friends, family, neighbors, coworkers, and fellow church members. It will revolutionize their understanding of God's assignment for their lives.

First, I want to thank God for inspiring me to pursue this project. I must also thank my faithful wife, Dr. Mildred Lowery, who has been at my side through all the trials and triumphs in my ministry. My son, Dr. Stephen Lowery, has worked with me diligently in the preparation of this manuscript. God has blessed me with a wonderful family who support me with their love and encouragement. Many of the staff at the National Church of God have been so helpful with their input and comments as they have read through this manuscript. I would also like to show my appreciation for my pastoral team, who labored with me in the research and editing process.

Please keep this book handy and refer to it often. I urge you not to miss one essential point. God will use you in an extraordinary way as you allow Him to manifest Himself through your life.

T. L. LOWERY, PH.D.

Chapter 1

THE HOLY SPIRIT TODAY

FOR MANY CENTURIES, the Holy Spirit was the forgotten person of the Trinity, and Pentecost was the much-neglected feast of the church. Thankfully, we can say this is no longer the case. God is revitalizing the entire church of the Lord Jesus Christ. The Holy Spirit, the third person of the Holy Trinity, manifests Himself in gatherings of every denomination. As Christian believers encounter the power of the Holy Spirit, they want to comprehend the gifts of the Spirit. This book serves as a guide to biblical principles and practical implications for the operation of spiritual gifts.

EXPLORING GOD'S GIFTS

Jesus described the Holy Spirit as the gift of the Father (John 14:26). Everything about Christianity is a gift. Our existence is a gift. Our talents are gifts. The environment in which we live is a gift. Salvation from the penalty of sin is a gift. New life in Christ is a gift.

Jesus comes to us as our Redeemer, saving us through His death on the cross. When we trust

Christ as our personal Savior and receive Him as our Lord, we are born again and become candidates for the baptism of the Holy Spirit.

RENEWAL IN THE BODY OF CHRIST

I grew up in a full-gospel, Pentecostal church. My father and mother were Spirit-filled ministers before I was born. My ministry and the churches to which I have ministered have consistently given honor to the Holy Spirit and recognized Him as a person. He is not just a gift, a manifestation, or a force. The Holy Spirit is God, a person of the Holy Trinity. I count myself fortunate to have been exposed to such a theological climate. I have had the privilege of sitting under and ministering to people who embrace the power of the Spirit.

God said through the Old Testament prophet Joel, *"I will pour out my Spirit on all people"* (Joel 2:28). We are seeing a fulfillment of that prophecy in the church today. I believe that we have seen the former or *"early"* rain. Now we are seeing the *"latter rain"* (James 5:7 KJV), the final great outpouring of the Holy Spirit. This divine visitation encompasses people of all denominations and cultures and is preparing the church, the body of Christ, for the coming of the Lord.

The emphasis on the *Pentecostal reality* has compelled major denominations to evaluate the vitality and strength of the renewal of the gifts of the Holy Spirit. *Pentecostal reality* is a term coined by Presbyterian charismatic theologian J. Rodman Williams to mean "the coming of God's Holy Spirit in power to the believing individual and community."[1] Pentecostal historian Vinson Synan writes:

> Around the world, denomination after denomination appointed study commissions to report on the charismatic movement, which now seemed to have entered into every congregation in Christendom....In general, these study reports...accepted the major premise of Pentecostalism, i.e., that the miraculous gifts of the Spirit did not cease after the apostolic age, but are even now demonstrated in the church by Spirit-filled believers.[2]

People are generally hungry for God's Word. Bible studies are flourishing. People desire to find biblical answers to their problems. Most Bible-believing Christians believe that the gifts of the Spirit are available for the people of God today. Many who once doubted that present-day Christians may experience certain spiritual *charisma,* or gifts, have changed their positions. The vast majority of evangelical Christians affirm that born-again believers need to be filled with the Spirit. As Peter Gillquist comments:

> Jesus is the *life* [Gillquist's emphasis]. Without the life, there's no living. His Holy Spirit provides life within us, the very life of God....In fact, if the life of the Holy Spirit isn't the central focus of the gathering, we wonder if we haven't wasted our time in coming....We have

lived in the mildewed atmosphere of dead or-
thodoxy, and now we hunger for the reality of
the life-giving Spirit....What we want is something alive.[3]

A restored emphasis on other biblical truths has
accompanied the renewal of spiritual gifts in the
Christian church. This naturally affects our overall
concept of faith and practice. As God's people, we
yearn to follow the biblical faith *"that was once for
all entrusted to the saints"* (Jude 3). In contrast to
those whom the spirit of the Antichrist seduces toward judgment, true believers long to follow the
voice of the Good Shepherd. (See John 10:14–16.)

As we seek to please God, we realize our need
for God's empowering. No one can please God in his
or her own strength. We must hunger and thirst after righteousness and fast and pray until God imparts to us the fullness of His Spirit. When this
happens in one's life, revival is a natural consequence. Jesus mandated that we preach and teach
the Gospel to the ends of the earth and make disciples. Being filled with the fullness of the Holy Spirit
will enable us to carry out His divine command.

SURVIVAL IN A HOSTILE ENVIRONMENT

Evidence of God's power is greatly needed today.
We live in a secular age, in which the majority of
people seem to have discounted the God of the Bible,
and view Him as irrelevant. They deny the funda-
mentals of the faith and have defaulted to the
teachings of agnostic and atheistic humanism.

Some have even turned to satanism and are worshipping Lucifer as god. Others have searched for truth in other religions of the world instead of in Christianity. These religious systems are incomplete and are totally unable to meet man's spiritual needs. They reach up to God but fall short each time.

Never before have the gifts of the Holy Spirit been so desperately needed in the church. The rhetoric of agnostic humanism and secularism seems feeble in the face of the grave difficulties humanity faces at the dawn of the third millennium. Only in Christianity does God reach down to humankind and offer the way to salvation. Authentic Christianity's inherent power and spiritual gifts are the answer to our generation's despair.

GOD'S DESIGN FOR SPIRITUAL GIFTS

We must always keep in mind that God did not give the gifts of the Spirit to help us impress others with how spiritual we are or for self-aggrandizement. Throughout the Scriptures, God says He will not share His glory with another. (See, for example, Isaiah 42:8.) The Lord provides the manifestations of the Holy Spirit to fulfill His purposes.

The implementation of the gifts of the Spirit edifies God's church in three ways. First, spiritual gifts enable individuals to develop in their spiritual growth. Secondly, God gives these gifts to build up the Christian community, the congregation of believers. Thirdly, the gifts are instruments that attract outsiders to faith in Christ. (See 1 Corinthians 14:1–26.)

THE FOUNDATION OF CHRISTIANITY

The great apostle Paul claimed that his message and preaching rested not on *"wise and persuasive words,"* but on *"a demonstration of the Spirit's power"* (1 Corinthians 2:4). The Christian faith is reasonable, yet it does not depend on faulty human reasoning. We have received *"the Spirit who is from God"* (v. 12) in order to understand what God has provided for us in Christ. Just as Peter's understanding of Jesus' identity was a revelation of the Father (Matthew 16:16–17), God continues to disclose things to His people, according to His Word.

BIBLICAL ACCOUNTS OF THE HOLY SPIRIT

When we examine any question, we should always turn to the Word of God. We find God's pattern for Christian living in the Bible. The book of Acts is the history of the early church, and we should ask ourselves this question about the experience of the first century believers: What distinguished the community of early Christians from all the other religious groups of their day? The answer is the unique, ongoing presence of the Holy Spirit. The Scriptures teach that the Spirit came to clothe, energize (Luke 24:49), and set up residence (1 John 2:27) in the followers of the risen Lord Jesus.

At Pentecost, God kept His promise to empower Christian believers to do His work. According to the Bible, the church is a group of people who are permeated and saturated with the Holy Spirit. This unusual proximity of God's Spirit results in signs, wonders, and demonstrations of divine power, and helps to endorse the church's message.

The power of the Holy Spirit is explosive. The Greek word for power is *dunamis*, from which we derive the English word *dynamite*. This power gives believers the force to win in spiritual battle and enlarge the extent of God's kingdom. *"The one who is in you is greater than the one who is in the world"* (1 John 4:4).

THE BIBLICAL DATA

Let us now briefly survey what the Scriptures say is the role of the Holy Spirit. It is important to recognize that the Holy Spirit is not a newcomer. He is the eternal third person of the Godhead. The Holy Spirit did not first arrive on earth on the Day of Pentecost. In Genesis 1:2, we find God's Spirit involved in the Creation of the earth. He is not simply a force, but He is God the Spirit. In describing the person and role of the Holy Spirit, I cannot stress enough that Christians do not believe in three Gods. The Bible teaches the existence of only one God (Deuteronomy 6:4). The Deity has revealed Himself as one God in three persons. The Scriptures instruct us that the Father is God, Jesus (the Word/Son) is God, and the Spirit is God; the Godhead consists of these three persons. The word *persons*, in this sense, does not mean personalities. In *Nelson's Introduction to the Christian Faith*, Klaas Runia writes, "One divine Personality exists in three different *personal* ways" (Runia's emphasis).[4]

The Holy Spirit is the Giver of Life. This title dates from the early centuries of the Christian church.[5] Wherever Scripture mentions the Spirit, it depicts Him in terms of "vitality, vibrancy, and movement," coming "to the rescue of humankind."[6]

John 15:26 says that the Holy Spirit comes to testify about Jesus. The Father has also sent Him to guide and empower us. The Holy Spirit enables us to become what God intended for us to become. He comes to make His home in us and restore our communion with our heavenly Father. Then, as the Spirit of God makes Himself visible through the manifestations, or gifts, of the Holy Spirit, others recognize God in our midst (1 Corinthians 14:24–25).

We must never lose sight of the fact that it is the Holy Spirit Himself who imparts the gifts as He wills. We should never attempt to manipulate the gifts of the Spirit. We do not control these gifts; we are Spirit-empowered believers and messengers of God, to be used by God to minister to the needs of the people (1 Corinthians 12:7).

THE SPIRIT IN THE OLD COVENANT

Throughout the pages of the Old Testament, we find many allusions to the Spirit of God. The pharaoh of Egypt referred to the Spirit of God (Genesis 41:38). God told Moses that His Spirit had empowered a craftsman named Bezalel to make items for Israel's holy place of worship (Exodus 31:2–5; 35:30–33).

When Moses needed help with his workload, God told Moses to bring to Him seventy of the nation's elders. He would *"take of the Spirit"* (Numbers 11:17) that was on Moses and put it on them. We find the Lord's Spirit active in the period of the judges and in the emergence of the monarchy in Israel. Evidence of the working of the Spirit is clearly found in the ministry of all the prophets, including John the Baptist.

THE SPIRIT IN THE NEW COVENANT

Without question, the Spirit of God accompanied Jesus of Nazareth. The Son and the Spirit were in communion with the Father when Jesus was on earth, as they are in communion with Him now. First John 2:27 teaches that followers of Jesus have received an anointing of the Spirit that remains. In the Old Testament, kings, priests, and prophets were anointed with oil as a sign that God had chosen them for specific tasks. In a similar way, God the Father gives the Holy Spirit to believers as His seal—as a guarantee of the eternal life they have already entered into (Ephesians 1:13–14).

Jesus commissioned His followers to *"make disciples of all nations"* (Matthew 28:19). He said that His authority to do this originated with the Father (v. 18). As the Father had sent Him, He was now sending His apostles (John 20:21). They had an assignment to carry on the ministry of Christ. Jesus said, *"I tell you the truth, anyone who has faith in me will do what I have been doing. He will do even greater things than these, because I am going to the Father"* (John 14:12).

God promised to *"put a new spirit"* (Ezekiel 11:19) in His people and to write His law on their hearts (Jeremiah 31:33). On the Day of Pentecost, God fulfilled His promise; believers received the power of the Holy Spirit, which enabled them not only to please God but also to do His work.

The book of Acts is a historical narrative of the Spirit's operation through God's people. Multitudes throughout the world turned to Christ as the apostles preached the Word and the Holy Spirit confirmed the message with signs and wonders.

In Ephesians, Paul described how God gives leadership to the church to help believers develop spiritually for the mission to which He calls them. In Romans, Paul explained how the Holy Spirit motivates believers in the direction of their callings. In 1 Corinthians 12–14, the apostle invested three intensive chapters to discuss the manifestations of the Holy Spirit and the implementation of these manifestations. Through His Word, God has provided us with a thorough Handbook to lead us in fulfilling His will for our lives.

SIGNS, WONDERS, AND THE EXPANSION OF CHRISTIANITY

"People are either missionaries or mission fields." This simple expression, made popular by international evangelist Tommy Lee Osborne, states the fact that all Christians have an evangelistic call on their lives. The Great Commission universally calls Christians to make disciples (Matthew 28:19). Jesus specifically linked the giving of the power of the Spirit with believers becoming His witnesses (Acts 1:8).

The early church preached a simple message, and it seemed absurd to those who heard it. Without the manifestations of the Spirit's presence, no one would have believed that the witness of the first Christians was credible. As we will discover in the next chapter, throughout the history of Christianity's expansion, signs and wonders have played a significant role. This was true of the work of apostolic missionaries such as Patrick in Ireland and Boniface in Germany. Reports indicate that miraculous signs also confirmed the preaching of Francis of Assisi, the great evangelist of the Middle Ages.

POWER FOR HEALING A BROKEN WORLD

Powerful manifestations of the Holy Spirit will convince secularists that there is something beyond that which can be verified in scientific experiments. The power of God can deliver those who are lost in the occult and every other satanic force of hell. Through the work of the Holy Spirit, we become the hands and mouth of Jesus to a world that is broken and hurting. To achieve the mission He has assigned to us, we must be filled with His Spirit and allow the gifts to be manifested in our lives.

In chapter three, I will discuss how you can be baptized in the Holy Spirit. But let us first see how the baptism and gifts of the Holy Spirit did not disappear with the early disciples but have been manifested throughout the church's history.

Notes

1. John Rodman Williams, *The Pentecostal Reality* (Plainfield, NJ: Logos International, 1972), 2.

2. Vinson Synan, *In the Latter Days: The Outpouring of the Holy Spirit in the Twentieth Century,* 2d ed. (Ann Arbor, MI: Servant Publications, 1991), 123, 126.

3. Peter E. Gillquist, *Let's Quit Fighting about the Holy Spirit* (Grand Rapids, MI: Zondervan Publishing House, 1974), 136.

4. Klaas Runia, "The Trinity," in *Nelson's Introduction to the Christian Faith,* ed. Robin Keeley (Nashville, TN: Thomas Nelson Publishers, 1992), 116.

5. The phrase calling the Holy Spirit the "Giver of Life" can be found most notably in the Niceno-Constantinopolitan Creed, whose third article begins, "I believe in the Holy Spirit, the Lord, the Giver of life." We popularly call this creed the Nicene Creed, although the statement of faith accepted at the Nicene Council in A.D. 325 was much shorter and only stated it believed in the Holy Spirit.

6. Clark H. Pinnock and Robert C. Brow, *Unbounded Love: A Good News Theology for the Twenty-First Century* (Downers Grove, IL: InterVarsity Press, 1994), 51.

Chapter 2

SPIRITUAL GIFTS IN CHURCH HISTORY

WE HAVE OBSERVED A great move of the Spirit recently, much like what happened in biblical times. But what about the period between the New Testament church and our day? Was the Holy Spirit totally inactive?

As we review church history, we find frequent references to extraordinary spiritual gifts in the lives of many great Christians as the church has expanded and experienced times of great revival. Those who deny the operation of certain spiritual gifts—especially tongues, prophecy, and gifts of healing—claim that such occurrences disappeared after the death of the apostles. No biblical assertion supports such an argument, and the historical evidence presents a different story.

THE PERIOD AFTER THE APOSTLES

From the writings of the early church Fathers, the Christian leaders who succeeded the apostles, it is clear that the activity of the Spirit continued. Bishop and martyr Ignatius (*c.* 35–*c.* 107) alluded to making a prophetic utterance.[1] Tertullian (*c.* 160–*c.* 225) distinguished himself as the first major theologian of early Christianity and defended orthodox Christianity against the erring Gnostics. In his writings, Tertullian informed his readers that spiritual gifts belong to the Christian experience.[2] Another great advocate of the faith, Justin Martyr (*c.* 100–*c.* 165), made similar comments.[3]

Irenaeus (*c.* 130–*c.* 200) was the Bishop of Lyons and a disciple of Polycarp, who was a disciple of the apostle John and an early Christian martyr. Irenaeus described those who prophesied and manifested Spirit-inspired languages as "spiritual people" who benefitted the Christian community.[4]

Origen (*c.* 185–254) spoke of the Spirit providing the "building blocks" upon which the Father energizes spiritual gifts. He understood that Jesus imparts and controls the operation of these gifts.[5] Origen highly regarded spiritual gifts, especially the word of wisdom and the word of knowledge.

ABUSES OF THE GIFTS

In the second half of the second century, the followers of Montanus of Phrygia exercised spiritual gifts. It frequently happens when the Spirit moves that Satan seeks to counterfeit God's work and sinful human nature strives to draw attention to itself. This appears to have been the case with the Montanists.

Although some genuine gifts of the Spirit may have been manifested among the Montanists, much of their activity took place in a state of trance. This meant that those who employed the so-called gifts were not in control of themselves but were "seized by a power beyond themselves."[6] In Scripture, those whom the Spirit truly led could exert self-control.

Eventually the leaders of the church judged this movement as heretical. Many prophets in the Montanist movement made prophecies that did not happen. One of these predicted the descent of the heavenly Jerusalem near Phrygia, the center of the Montanist movement.[7] Unfortunately, this situation drove church officials to view as suspect all spiritual or supernatural activity. A more conservative, institutional approach in governing the church seemed a safer route to take. Rather than seeking to discern the true source of inspiration, much of the church forsook the gifts of the Spirit altogether.

CONTINUED APPEARANCES OF THE GIFTS

Despite the caution exhibited in leadership circles, the Spirit continued to express Himself in the building of the church. Reports persisted regarding the operation of the gifts of the Spirit through various individuals. These include the Roman elder and martyr Novatian (c. 250), Bishop Hilary of Poitiers (c. 315–67), and Bishop Ambrose of Milan (c. 339–97). Contemporaries referred to Ephraem of Syria (c. 306–73), a theologian of the Eastern church, as the "Harp of the Spirit." He credited the Spirit with bringing about meaningful worship. Assyrian Christian thinker Narsai (d. *c.* 503) also placed great emphasis on the operation of the Spirit in the church.[8] We find examples of the various workings of the Spirit in the lives of the monastics, the missionaries, and many other exemplary Christians.

Though we hear little of the manifestations of the Spirit during the Middle Ages, miraculous acts were reported in the lives of people such as Dominic, Hildegard of Bingen, Joachim of Flora, Francis of Assisi, and Antony of Padua.[9]

THE REFORMATION

During the late Middle Ages, another gospel infiltrated the Christian church in the West. Some church leaders promoted a system of "works" that supposedly led to God. That system made these leaders influential but terrorized the ordinary Christian. Failing to teach the grace of God, spiritual shepherds misguided and impoverished the Christian believers. Thankfully, Jesus promised that the Spirit would come to teach us and guide us into all truth. Whenever God's people lose their way, God sends prophets to correct them. In this case, the Reformation resulted.

Godly Bible students recognized something was amiss. John Huss (*c.* 1372–1415) attempted to restore biblical Christianity. He was accused of heresy and was executed. Huss was not alone in giving his life for the reformation of the church.

Finally, a brave theologian, priest, and monk named Martin Luther (1483–1546) waged a war of ideas against a system that had become Christian in name only. Luther helped the church rediscover the truth that God's grace alone, through faith, saves the lost (Romans 1:17). Good works do not save us, although our salvation will result in good works (Ephesians 2:8–10). Luther believed and taught that every believer could receive spiritual gifts.[10]

John Calvin (1509–64) was a gifted Reformation theologian who focused on God's sovereignty. Calvin described speaking in tongues in the early church as an "adornment and honor of the Gospel itself."[11]

During the Reformation, the Anabaptist leader Menno Simons (1496–1561) wrote about the gifts of the Spirit with spiritual understanding. In addition, speaking in tongues and other manifestations were well known among the Moravian Brethren. The French Camisards practiced the spiritual gifts, seeing them as a further fulfillment of Joel's prophecy.[12] A renewed interest in biblical study led many to desire the experience of the early church.

THE GREAT AWAKENINGS AND METHODISM

Around 1726, a great spiritual awakening of interest in the Christian faith began in the United States through the preaching of Jonathan Edwards (1703–58) and others.[13] In this Great Awakening, people experienced extraordinary manifestations of the Spirit.

In England in 1738, Anglican priest John Wesley (1703–91) came into a personal relationship with Christ and sought to bring New Testament "methods" to the church of his day. He preached that there was yet another spiritual experience after conversion and believed in the perpetuity of spiritual gifts, including the gift of tongues.[14] Home meetings and Bible study characterized the Methodist movement. Despite John Wesley's desire that this movement bring renewal within the Anglican Church, it eventually became its own denomination.

British preacher George Whitefield (1714–70), an associate of Wesley's, participated substantially in the American revival. Observers widely reported manifestations of the Spirit in meetings he conducted. Such phenomena continued to appear in the Second Great Awakening, which began at the end of the eighteenth century.

THE HOLINESS AND DEEPER LIFE MOVEMENTS

The Holiness Movement in the 1800s placed great focus on the need for God's people to be consecrated for service and separated from the evils of this world. A new longing for God's sanctifying power was born. In addition to having a personal relationship with God, people wanted to live holy lives as examples of God's grace.

Manifestations of the Spirit were important elements in the Cane Ridge Revival, the meetings of Charles Grandison Finney, the Shaker movement, and Edward Irving's Catholic Apostolic Church.

People yearned for more of God. Finney said ministers had no right to be in the pulpit unless they had been "endued with power from on high."[15] Intellectual discussions about God and His nature failed to satisfy the spiritual hunger of the people. They wanted to experience a personal and genuine relationship with Christ.

Such desires led to the formation of the Deeper Life movement of the nineteenth century. Numerous revival movements made the rediscovery of the Pentecostal reality possible for vast numbers of the Christian church. Men like Dwight Lyman Moody, Reuben Archer Torrey, and Albert Benjamin Simpson preached the necessity of a baptism of the Spirit that would give one the spiritual preparation to serve God.[16]

THE PENTECOSTAL REVOLUTION

As we move in our survey toward the twentieth century, we find increasing interest in the fullness of the Spirit and the exercise of all the gifts of the Spirit listed in Scripture. During and after the so-called Age of Enlightenment (eighteenth century), reason and science were made gods. Skeptics attacked religion and seduced a number of fearful church leaders to abandon biblical Christianity. This created a great thirst among many believers to see a return of the power they read about in the pages of the New Testament. Christians of all denominations had a reawakened interest in the Spirit and the gifts of the Spirit.[17]

Central to the revived attention being paid to spiritual gifts was a connection between speaking in tongues and the baptism in the Holy Spirit. In 1896, tongues were reportedly manifested in meetings of a group called the Christian Union. This later became the Church of God, Cleveland, Tennessee.[18] The Church of God is able to claim itself as the oldest of the Pentecostal denominations.[19]

A major landmark in the explosion of spiritual gifts took place at the Bethel Bible School in Topeka, Kansas. The students of Charles Parham had concluded, after an extensive review of the biblical materials, that speaking in tongues was the "indisputable proof" of spiritual baptism.[20] Later Pentecostals would speak of tongues as the "initial evidence" of the baptism in the Holy Spirit.

During a watchnight service that started on the last night of 1900, one student, Agnes Ozman, asked Parham to lay hands on her and pray for her to receive the baptism in the Holy Spirit with the evidence of speaking in tongues. As she received the baptism, she spoke in what was reportedly the Chinese language. On January 1, 1901, newspapers declared, "Pentecost in Topeka, Kansas." Additional accounts recorded that within a few days after Agnes Ozman's experience, others also spoke in tongues.[21]

In 1906, William Seymour, an African-American Holiness minister, started preaching the Pentecostal message he had received from Charles Parham. Neely Terry, a Holiness pastor, invited Seymour to speak at her church in Los Angeles. When Seymour taught that the gift of speaking in tongues was the initial evidence of being baptized in the Holy Spirit, Terry asked him to leave. The interesting thing was that Seymour himself had yet to experience the manifestation of tongues. He continued to preach in home meetings there. A very young African-American boy was the first to receive the experience. Eventually, Seymour rented and ministered at an old Methodist church at 312 Azusa Street in Los Angeles, and the great Azusa Street Revival resulted. These meetings lasted for three years. From here, the Pentecostal movement spread around the world.[22]

While authentic gifts of the Spirit flourished in this revival, some abuses arose. The church at Corinth, and later the Montanists, had experienced similar occurrences of error. At first, many mainline churches expelled those who propagated Pentecostal teaching, fearing that Pentecostalism was extreme emotionalism. The situation brought about the formation of many Pentecostal denominations.

The outbreak of charismatic gifts was not limited to America. Pentecostal leader David du Plessis said, regarding the Pentecostal and charismatic renewals, "In the beginning I heard the preachers in the historic churches say, 'Don't worry. It is just a passing wind. It will soon blow over.' And it did—it blew all over!"[23]

In the Welsh revivals of the early 1900s, tongues and other remarkable demonstrations of the Spirit were evident. Other great moves of the Spirit took place in England, South Africa, Norway, India, Russia, Chile, and Brazil. The message of Pentecost continued to progress across Latin America and Western Europe.[24] Demos Shakarian, founder of the Full Gospel Business Men's Fellowship International, often pointed to the charismatic revival in Armenia as a divine turning point for his family.[25]

NEO-PENTECOSTALS, CHARISMATICS, AND THIRD WAVE EVANGELICALS

Around the middle of the twentieth century, people from mainline denominations began experiencing the reality of all of the spiritual gifts, commencing the Neo-Pentecostal movement. Harald Bredesen, a Lutheran pastor, and Dennis Bennett, an Episcopalian priest, shocked their congregations with the news that they had experienced the gifts of the Holy Spirit, including the gift of tongues.[26]

The message of the power of the Spirit spread to every denomination, including the ancient Catholic and Orthodox churches. Various conservative evangelicals, once cautious about Pentecostalism, have come to actively pursue manifestations of the Spirit. This movement, described by some as the Third Wave, consists of evangelicals who believe in the continuation of spiritual gifts but do not necessarily embrace all elements of Pentecostal and charismatic theology.[27]

THE CHURCH: THE PEOPLE OF THE SPIRIT

While the Holy Spirit has been at work throughout the church age, God is certainly recharging

Christians with the power of the Holy Spirit in our day. The Reformation restored the truths of salvation by grace through faith and the priesthood of all believers to their central position in the Christian faith. The Wesleyan Revival focused on the importance of a personal relationship with Christ. The Holiness Movement reminded us that our lives are to be consecrated to God's service. In the same way, the Pentecostal movement and the charismatic renewal have illuminated essential tools for a continuing vital Christianity.

This renewal emphasized the lordship of Christ, Bible study, small group meetings, and encountering God's presence in worship. The church can now function more fully as God intended. A church is not a one-man band. Christian service is an orchestra with God as the Conductor. He directs the work of His people with the gifts of the Holy Spirit, which He places in the church.

Notes

1. J. B. Lightfoot and J. R. Harmer, eds., *The Apostolic Fathers* (Grand Rapids, MI: Baker Book House, 1956), 80–81.

2. George H. Williams and Edith Waldvogel, "A History of Speaking in Tongues and Related Gifts," in *The Charismatic Movement,* ed. Michael P. Hamilton (Grand Rapids, MI: William B. Eerdmans Publishing Company, 1975), 66.

3. Charles G. Hummel, *Fire in the Fireplace: Contemporary Charismatic Renewal* (Downers Grove, IL: InterVarsity Press, 1978), 164.

4. Williams and Waldvogel, "Speaking in Tongues," 20–21.

5. Cecil M. Robeck, Jr., "Origen's Treatment of the Charismata in 1 Corinthians 12:8–10," in *Charismatic Experiences in History,* ed. Cecil M. Robeck, Jr. (Peabody, MA: Hendrickson Publishers, 1985), 112.

6. Josephine Massyngberde Ford, "The Charismatic Gifts in Worship," in *The Charismatic Movement,* ed. Michael P. Hamilton (Grand Rapids, MI: William B. Eerdmans Publishing Company, 1975), 114.

7. "Montanism," in *The Oxford Dictionary of the Christian Church,* ed. Frank Leslie Cross and Elizabeth Anne Livingstone (Oxford: Oxford University Press, 1974), 934.

8. Stanley M. Burgess, "Doctrine of the Holy Spirit: The Ancient Fathers," in *Dictionary of Pentecostal and Charismatic Movements,* ed. Stanley M. Burgess, Gary B. McGee, and Patrick H. Alexander (Grand Rapids, MI: Zondervan Publishing House, 1988), 426–429.

9. For a more complete account of the work of the Spirit in the Middle Ages, see George H. Williams and Edith Waldvogel, "A History of Speaking in Tongues and Related Gifts," in *The Charismatic Movement,* ed. Michael P.

Hamilton (Grand Rapids, MI: William B. Eerdmans Publishing Company, 1975), 67–71.

10. Williams and Waldvogel, "Speaking in Tongues," 71–72.

11. Ibid., 73.

12. Ibid., 71–77.

13. See "Jonathan Edwards," in *The Oxford Dictionary of the Christian Church*, ed. Frank Leslie Cross and Elizabeth Anne Livingstone (Oxford: Oxford University Press, 1974), 446. See also Francis MacNutt, *Overcome by the Spirit* (Old Tappan, NJ: Chosen Books, 1990), 101–103.

14. Williams and Waldvogel, "Speaking in Tongues," 80.

15. Charles Grandison Finney, *Power from on High* (Ft. Washington, PA: Christian Literature Crusade, 1949), 21.

16. Reuben Archer Torrey clearly outlines this position in his book, *The Baptism with the Holy Spirit* (Minneapolis, MN: Dimension Books, 1972).

17. Vinson Synan, *In the Latter Days: The Outpouring of the Holy Spirit in the Twentieth Century*, 2d ed. (Ann Arbor, MI: Servant Publications, 1991), 42.

18. Vinson Synan, *The Twentieth Century Pentecostal Explosion: The Exciting Growth of Pentecostal Churches and Charismatic Renewal Movements* (Altamonte Springs, FL: Creation House, 1987), 67.

19. Williams and Waldvogel, "Speaking in Tongues," 95.

20. Ibid., 97.

21. Synan, *In the Latter Days*, 47.

22. Walter J. Hollenweger, *The Pentecostals* (Minneapolis, MN: Augsburg Publishing House, 1972), 23–24.

23. David Johannes du Plessis, "Holy Spirit in Ecumenical Movement," in *Jesus, Where Are You Taking Us?: Messages from the First International Lutheran Conference on the Holy Spirit*, ed. Norris Wogen (Carol

Stream, IL: Creation House, 1973), 225.

24. Vinson Synan, *In the Latter Days,* 55ff.

25. Demos Shakarian, John L. Sherrill, and Elizabeth Sherrill, *The Happiest People on Earth* (Lincoln, VA: Chosen Books, 1975), 15–27.

26. John L. Sherrill, *They Speak with Other Tongues* (Old Tappan, NJ: Spire Books, 1964), 17, 62.

27. For an overview of these various movements, see Vinson Synan, *The Twentieth Century Pentecostal Explosion: The Exciting Growth of Pentecostal Churches and Charismatic Renewal Movements* (Altamonte Springs, FL: Creation House, 1987). The amazing story of how God led Brother David du Plessis to help open the doors for the Pentecostal experience in many denominations is found in his book, *The Spirit Bade Me Go* (Plainfield, NJ: Logos International, 1977). For the complete stories of Harald Bredesen and Dennis Bennett, see Harald Bredesen and Pat King, *Yes, Lord* (Plainfield, NJ: Logos International, 1972) and Dennis Joseph Bennett, *Nine O'Clock in the Morning* (Plainfield, NJ: Logos International, 1970). For information on the Catholic charismatic renewal, see Kilian McDonnell, ed., *The Holy Spirit and Power: The Catholic Charismatic Renewal* (Garden City, NY: Doubleday, 1975). For more information about the Third Wave, see Charles Peter Wagner, *The Third Wave of the Holy Spirit* (Ann Arbor, MI: Vine Books, 1988).

Chapter 3

BAPTIZED IN THE HOLY SPIRIT

H OW CAN WE describe an encounter with almighty God, the One who made the heavens and earth? What phrase can we employ to explain our interaction with the Creator of all things? Human words fall far short of expressing or enabling us to comprehend who God is and how He makes Himself known to us. The apostle Paul compares our understanding of the things of God to a person using a piece of polished metal, such as brass, to view his own reflection (1 Corinthians 13:12). Nothing looks clear; everything is somewhat distorted. Detecting the details is difficult, if possible at all. In the same way, Christians *"know in part and...prophesy in part"* (v. 9). Since this is the case, how do we come to know God and receive all that He has for us?

GOD'S GREATEST GIFT: THE NEW BIRTH

The absolute prerequisite for spiritual power is to be *"born again"* (John 3:3). The new birth is the gateway through which all other spiritual blessings are received. To understand the new birth, we must turn to the third chapter of the book of John. In this passage, Jesus says one must be born again to perceive and enter the kingdom of God (v. 3). He said this to Nicodemus, a spiritual leader of the Jews and a respected teacher of the law. Then He stated that the workings of the Spirit are mysterious and supernatural. Jesus said that we cannot see the Spirit Himself, but we can see the results of His work. We cannot see the breeze, but we can feel the rushing air and see the leaves of the trees move. The wind comes and goes, but though we hear it, we do not know *where it comes from or where it is going. So it is with everyone born of the Spirit"* (v. 8).

Jesus taught that God loves us and created us for a purpose. We are not here by accident. God made us. He formed us. We are the apple of His eye (Deuteronomy 32:10). We are His handiwork, His masterpiece, His Rembrandt. But the only way for us to reach our maximum potential is to be born again. All humanity has sinned against God and has broken relationship with Him. Because of man's sin, he is unable to find God's purpose in life or understand God's love. However, God offers a solution to this: the new birth. If we place our trust in Jesus as our Savior and Lord, God delivers us from our sins. We are born again from above. We become members of God's family. We have a home in heaven when we die.

I have been in church all my life. The earliest thing I can remember is being in church. Yet this did not automatically make me a Christian. I had to personally accept Christ into my life and surrender to

His lordship. Since being born again is essential for salvation and receiving the baptism in the Holy Spirit, I would like to share with you how I became a Christian.

I received Christ as my Savior when I was fourteen years of age. The Reverend W. G. Abney, a young Church of God pastor, came to Warner Robins, Georgia, and started a mission. Although my parents belonged to another denomination, they assisted him in getting a church started.

One Sunday evening, while this man of God was preaching, the Holy Spirit convicted me as I stood in the back of that little mission, which was meeting in an Army barracks. When he finished his message, I ran down to the altar to surrender my heart to the Lord. My parents and other believers came around me and started praying for me, and the Lord saved me. He gave me a vision of myself climbing up a steep hill. The hill was so steep that I was pulling at the shrubs and bushes, trying to reach the top. When I got to the top of that hill, I looked up and saw Christ on the cross. I saw His blood dripping from His hands, side, and feet, and from the wounds caused by the crown of thorns on His head. Then I witnessed the Lord writing my name in a book, Thomas Lanier Lowery.

There aren't enough devils in hell or on earth, loosed or bound, that could ever make me doubt my relationship with God. The Word of God says in Romans 10:9–10:

> *If you confess with your mouth, "Jesus is Lord," and believe in your heart that God raised him from the dead, you will be saved. For it is with your heart that you believe and are justified, and it is with your mouth that you confess and are saved.*

That is all that is necessary. Salvation transforms us into temples of the Holy Spirit (1 Corinthians 6:19).

JESUS: THE BAPTIZER IN THE HOLY SPIRIT

The writers of the Bible made it plain that God gives power to believers. They used various terms to express this truth: *immersion, fullness, fire,* and *endued.* Through our survey of church history, we discovered that believers throughout the ages have availed themselves of God's infinite spiritual resources. The question now is, "How do we appropriate the power God wants to give us?"

The word *baptize* is quite descriptive of what the Holy Spirit does when He fills believers. It means to "immerse, plunge, submerge, or inundate." God wants to overwhelm us with His Spirit.

In Isaiah 4:2, the prophet described the coming Messiah as the *"Branch of the LORD."* The prophecy foretold that the Messiah would cleanse *"by a spirit of judgment and a spirit of fire"* (v. 4). In the Gospels, we observe John the Baptist returning to this theme. He described the One who would saturate with "the Holy Breath and fire," in terms of judgment.[1]

Baptized in the Holy Spirit

At His ascension, Christ assured His followers that the gift of the Father would come. The risen Lord used an analogy to describe this gift: God would clothe believers with heavenly power. As Jesus baptizes us in the Holy Spirit, a release of God's power is activated in our lives. Suddenly, we find God's love made visible in our midst by what we commonly call the gifts of the Holy Spirit. These supernatural exhibitions of God's presence, manifested through willing followers of Christ, are extensions of God's grace and love. They enable us to complete the missions God assigns us, individually and corporately.

PENTECOST AS A PRESENT REALITY

While the Holy Spirit indwells all Christians, we know that not all Christians have been baptized in the Holy Spirit. Many wonderful Christians go through their whole lives attending church and serving God, and yet find themselves powerless. How do we receive the power from on high?

First, we must confess all known sins. If we agree with the Holy Spirit regarding sins He brings to our attention and confess our sins to God, we have the promise that He is *"faithful and just and will forgive us our sins and purify us from all unrighteousness"* (1 John 1:9).

Next, we must obey God in all things. We must follow the example and instruction of the Lord regarding water baptism and regularly gather with other believers in the worship of God.

Beyond all these, there is yet another require-
ment. Jesus said that we must ask! The Word of God
says, *"Your Father in heaven* [will] *give good gifts to
those who ask him!"* (Matthew 7:11). It is God's will
that all believers possess the power of the Holy
Spirit. It is not the domain of some special, elite
class in God's kingdom, but it is for all who ask.

At this point, many people get confused over
semantics. Pentecostals speak of being "baptized in
(or, with) the Holy Spirit."[2] This is a biblical expression. Jesus used this term when He referred to the
initial outpouring of the Spirit (Acts 1:5), which fulfilled the prophecy of John the Baptist (Matthew
3:11). Jesus baptizes the believer in the Holy Spirit
and imparts the power of God into his life for Christian service. The believer no longer relies on his own
might but on God's infinite strength.

Some refer to the baptism in the Holy Spirit as
being "filled with the Spirit."[3] This is a perfect description. To be filled with God's Spirit is to be controlled and empowered by Him. When we describe a
town as being "filled with rage," we mean that rage
has taken control of the people of that town. If we
say someone is "filled with wine," we mean that the
wine has intoxicated that person; he is under the
control of the wine. According to Scripture, to be
filled with wine is, at best, a waste of time and, at
worst, an extremely destructive activity (Ephesians
5:18). Rather, Scripture commands all Christians to
"be filled with the Spirit" (v. 18). The Greek word
Paul used here actually connotes, "keep on being
filled with the Spirit." Once Jesus baptizes us in the

Spirit, the anointing remains. However, we must continually strive to relinquish our wills to the Lord to keep on being filled with the Spirit.

We must be careful about using the misleading description "infilling" to describe being filled with the Spirit, as if it is a process in which we are "filled up" with the Spirit over a period of time. First, *infilling* is not a biblical term. Secondly, we do not receive part of the Spirit. The Spirit is a whole person; we cannot receive Him in percentages. His anointing is either there or it is not. *Filled*, rather than *infilling,* is the proper term.

Before the Day of Pentecost, Jesus commanded the disciples to *"tarry"* (Luke 24:49 KJV) in Jerusalem and await the promise of the Father. Some people think it is still necessary to tarry, but the wait is over.[4] The Comforter has come! No one has had to tarry since the Day of Pentecost. The Scripture says, *"Receive ye the Holy Ghost"* (John 20:22 KJV).

Let me return briefly to my personal testimony to illustrate this point. After receiving Christ as my personal Savior, I sought Him for deliverance from my old sin nature through a deeper sanctifying experience. The moment I realized this marvelous experience, I received a fullness of joy I had not imagined possible. Then I began to seek the baptism of the Holy Spirit. In those days, we had been taught that being filled with the Holy Spirit was an extended process of seeking and tarrying. We went to the altar, raised our hands, and said, "Glory, Glory, Glory." We thought that if we persisted long enough, the Holy Spirit would come upon us and baptize us. With that mentality, I began to seek the Lord to fill me with the Spirit.

I sought the Lord for a period of time, but nothing happened. I went away to attend Bible college and continued to seek the Lord to fill me with His Spirit. But again, nothing happened. Finally, I returned to the little mission church where I had been converted, and there the Lord marvelously baptized me with the Holy Spirit. I didn't have to wait long. The night I received the Holy Spirit baptism, I felt such an awesome presence of God and spoke with tongues for several hours.

If you are a Christian but have never been baptized in the Spirit, I urge you, in the name of Jesus, to be filled with the Holy Spirit. You do not need to wait any longer for this release of God's power. It is available to all believers in the name of Jesus. Delight in the Lord! Receive from Him all that He has for you! This release of the Holy Spirit is a gateway to fulfilling the call God has on your life in His power.

Notes

1. Donald L. Gelpi, S. J., "Breath-Baptism in the Synoptics," in *Charismatic Experiences in History,* ed. Cecil M. Robeck, Jr. (Peabody, MA: Henrickson Publishers, 1985), 16. Gelpi notes that John the Baptist's "phrase, 'to baptize in a Holy Breath,' described metaphorically God's sanctifying activity in the age which was about to dawn. The 'Mightier One' would send the divine Breath to cleanse the repentant of their sinfulness."

2. For a full discussion of the different uses of the term "baptized in the Holy Spirit" by Luke and Paul, see Roger Stronstad, *The Charismatic Theology of St. Luke* (Peabody, MA: Hendrickson Publishers, 1984) and Charles G. Hummel, *Fire in the Fireplace: Contemporary Charismatic Renewal* (Downers Grove, IL: InterVarsity Press, 1978). Peter E. Gillquist, evangelical writer and founder of the Evangelical Orthodox Church, pleads for Christians to seek the reality of the Holy Spirit's power and to stop fighting over semantics in *Let's Quit Fighting about the Holy Spirit* (Grand Rapids, MI: Zondervan Publishing House, 1974).

3. Some object to using the term "baptism in the Spirit" because they feel it is confusing. See James Douglas Grant Dunn, *Baptism in the Holy Spirit: A Re-Examination of the New Testament Teaching on the Gift of the Spirit in Relation to Pentecostalism Today* (Philadelphia: The Westminster Press, 1970); John R. W. Stott, *Baptism and Fullness: The Work of the Holy Spirit Today,* 2d. ed. (Downers Grove, IL: InterVarsity Press, 1976); John F. MacArthur, Jr., *Charismatic Chaos* (Grand Rapids, MI: Zondervan Publishing House, 1992); and Frederick Dale Bruner, *A Theology of the Holy Spirit: The Pentecostal Experience and the New Testament Witness* (Grand Rapids, MI: William B. Eerdmans Publishing Company, 1970). For a theological response to some of these objections from a charismatic perspective, see Howard Matthew Ervin, *Conversion-Initiation and the Baptism in the Holy Spirit*

(Peabody, MA: Hendrickson Publishers, 1987).

The apostle Paul speaks of being baptized *"by one Spirit into one body"* (1 Corinthians 12:13) at conversion. The Greek phrase also could be translated "in one Spirit." This refers to the moment when we are incorporated into the body of Christ. This baptism is the spiritual baptism into Christ's church, not the release of power referred to in Acts. According to John's gospel, the apostles had already received the Spirit on the evening of the Resurrection (John 20:22). They were born again at that point but did not receive power for ministry until the Day of Pentecost.

4. J. E. Stiles strongly emphasizes this point in his book, *The Gift of the Holy Spirit* (Glendale, CA: The Church Press, n.d.), 104–105.

Chapter 4

GIFTED TO SERVE IN MINISTRY

I N THE NEW TESTAMENT, we fail to find a highly developed church hierarchy. Each local assembly was a gathering of brothers and sisters in Christ, all related to each other by their commitment to the risen Lord. God has established leadership within the church, but He appoints all believers to the task of the ministry.

The apostle Paul taught that after Christ's ascension, He gave gifts of leadership to the church (Ephesians 4:8, 11–12). In verse eight, Paul uniquely used the Greek word *domata* to describe these gifts.[1] The gifts of leadership are apostle, prophet, evangelist, and pastor-teacher. Jesus gave these servant-leaders to the church to prepare the whole Christian community for the work of the ministry.

The word *minister* means "servant." Leaders are appointed in order to help believers fulfill their individual ministries. Jesus Himself taught that leaders in the Christian faith are required to be servants. On one occasion, He called His disciples together and said:

You know that the rulers of the Gentiles lord it over them, and their high officials exercise authority over them. Not so with you. Instead, whoever wants to become great among you must be your servant, and whoever wants to be first must be your slave—just as the Son of Man did not come to be served, but to serve, and to give his life as a ransom for many.

(Matthew 20:25–28)

Early Christians never said, "Let the pastor do it." Every believer had experienced an electrifying encounter with the Holy Spirit. All Christians knew that God had plans for their lives. The Lord gave leadership gifts so that the people of God could move toward maturity and serve wisely. God assigned Christian leaders the task of *"equipping...the saints"* (Ephesians 4:12 NKJV) for the work of the Lord.[2]

Therefore, ministry, from the beginning of the church, was the task of all believers, not just an elite few. All Christian believers testified about their faith to those they met. All of them prayed for their friends and families. God healed the sick and saved many as a result of the ministry of ordinary Christians. God was the source of their power for witnessing and service.

In this chapter, we will explore the ways in which those with leadership gifts help to equip the saints for the work of the Lord. To begin with, in every sense, leaders are to follow the example of Jesus. Jesus recruited, trained, and deployed those who were to lead His people. So today, Christian leaders are to multiply themselves in others, teaching people not only how to live the Christian life but how to help others as well.

LEADERSHIP GIFTS TO THE CHURCH

The early church followed the model of the Jewish synagogue. Seasoned people of integrity led the congregation. These elders were respected examples to follow. They dispensed wise counsel. They were responsible for leading public worship. Christian leaders used this pattern in providing a structure for simplifying the church's task.

Paul identified five leadership ministries in Ephesians 4:11. What was the purpose of each of these ministries?

Apostle

Paul listed the role of apostle first. An *apostle* in the ancient world was simply an emissary, a representative, one sent by another. Christ had especially selected a group of men to guard the foundation of the faith. We know these men as the Twelve.[3] The risen Christ also added Paul to the list of this authoritative group. The apostles were Christ's representatives and guardians of the faith. All except Paul had been with Jesus during His earthly ministry.

New Testament believers used the word *apostle* in a broader sense. Such apostles were pioneers—missionaries. Christ continues to equip the church with this kind of minister today. An apostle ventures into new frontiers, bringing the Gospel and planting churches in previously unreached areas. While these ministers have a great assignment, they do not have the apostolic authority of the Twelve or the apostle Paul. Paul was so concerned about preserving the true message of the Gospel that he wrote vehemently, *"Even if we or an angel from heaven should preach a gospel other than the one we preached to you, let him be eternally condemned!"* (Galatians 1:8). All Christian leaders today, even those who function in the role of apostle, are subject to the authority of the Gospel, as it is recorded in Holy Scripture. Jude referred to the Gospel as *"the faith that was once for all entrusted to the saints"* (Jude 3).

Prophet

Paul described the second ministry gift as that of prophet. While all believers may prophesy when moved upon by the Holy Spirit, Christ gives to the church certain individuals who can clearly hear God's word and speak it prophetically. When errors creep into the church or sins infect believers, it is often the prophet who brings light to the situation. The prophet is the one who frequently takes the first stand in opposing society's ills.

Evangelist

Christ bestowed a third ministry gift to the church, that of evangelist. Evangelists are those especially gifted to express the Gospel in such a way that people are led into a relationship with God through Jesus Christ. In the book of Acts, Philip was just such an evangelist. He led the expansion of Christianity into Samaria (Acts 8:5–8) and converted an Ethiopian official (vv. 26–39).

Pastor-Teacher

The last ministry gift Paul listed is the gift of pastor-teacher. Some separate this combination. Other biblical scholars think that these two go together and are simply two parts of a single ministry. A pastor is a shepherd—one who leads, feeds, and protects his flock. Other designations for Christian leadership include "overseer" and "elder." The New Testament requires a Christian leader to lead by example as well as through words. The ministry gift of teacher describes one who faithfully transmits the tenets of the Christian faith, interprets them in light of contemporary situations, and trains believers in living the Christian faith.[4] Seeking the Lord in prayer and studying God's Word are responsibilities of all ministers of the Word so that they will find direction for God's people (Acts 6:1–7).

MINISTRY GIFTS AND SPIRITUAL GIFTS

How do ministry gifts relate to the gifts of the Spirit? First, spiritual gifts aid the five leadership ministries in accomplishing their tasks. God does not so much assign a believer to a spiritual office as He permits the believer to function in a certain area.[5] If someone serves as a shepherd, he is a shepherd. An evangelist is someone who is leading people to Jesus.

Secondly, leaders, as a part of their roles in equipping the saints, are to teach others how the gifts of the Holy Spirit are to function. In the New Testament, we see that there was an expectation that every believer become a responsible worker in the Christian vineyard.

Moreover, leaders and all of God's people receive graces of the Spirit, which we sometimes call "motivational gifts." (See Romans 12:6–8.) As we will discover in a later chapter, these gifts direct all of God's people toward the mission of their lives. Paul taught that all members of the body of Christ are equally important, even if their roles differ (1 Corinthians 12).

EVERY BELIEVER HAS A UNIQUE ASSIGNMENT

As we progress in our study of spiritual gifts, it is important for us to remember that each of us has a unique call. I have sensed God's leading in my life. I have also seen God's clear call on the lives of many other people. On the night the Lord saved me, I immediately stood up and announced, "The Lord has called me to preach." There had been a desire upon my heart to preach from my earliest childhood. After I was saved and called to the ministry, my mother told me that before I was born, the Lord had revealed to her that she would have a son who would preach the Gospel around the world. God has fulfilled that promise. Over the course of my life, I have had the privilege of preaching in many different countries, on every continent.

Again, God has called every believer to a particular assignment. Every person's call is unique and different. I cannot carry out your mission; you cannot accomplish mine. While we may admire others in their zeal and service for Christ, we must seek to follow the route God has chosen for us. This route may take a variety of directions.

For example, during different stages in my life, the Lord has led me to minister in various capacities. I have been a pastor, an evangelist, and an administrator of many churches. While I was attending college, I was appointed to pastor a little country church near the college. This opportunity gave me excellent experience in the ministry at an early age.

God often uses circumstances to direct us. While I was in college, I met Mildred, the wonderful lady who would become my wife. Her father was pastoring in West Virginia. After I finished college, I began to conduct revivals for him and other pastors until Mildred and I were married. After we were married, we pastored for four or five years.

The burden for evangelism became so strong upon my heart that I resigned a very prosperous pastorate, purchased a large tent, and began conducting mass crusades across the nation. I did this for seventeen years, and I loved every minute of it. But God changed the direction of my ministry again. I was called to pastor the North Cleveland Church of God in Cleveland, Tennessee. For the next five years, as pastor of that church, the Lord gave us tremendous growth. During my tenure, we built a new sanctuary, a retirement complex for the elderly, and added approximately fifteen hundred new members to the church.

In 1974, I was elected assistant general overseer of my denomination, and I served there for the next eight years. During a forty-day fast, I was led by God to become pastor of the National Church of God in Washington, D.C. It has become one of the fastest growing churches in America. It is amazing how God will divinely and sovereignly direct our lives if we will submit to His will.

In a congregation patterned after New Testament examples, everyone should function in a ministry and manifest the gifts of the Spirit. How did the early church grow? "Each one would tell one."[6] Everybody was a witness. There were no spectators on the sidelines. The early Christians did not appeal to elaborate logic. They simply told what God had done in their lives. When someone was sick, they prayed for healing. When God healed and performed a miracle, it became a marvelous opportunity to share the Gospel. In contemporary Christianity as well, we must all seek to be ambassadors of Christ (2 Corinthians 5:20).

Notes

1. B. E. Underwood, *Spiritual Gifts: Ministries and Manifestations* (Franklin Springs, GA: Advocate Press, 1984), 11.

2. For an excellent resource on this subject, see Michael Harper, *Let My People Grow: Ministry and Leadership in the Church* (Plainfield, NJ: Logos International, 1977).

3. Jesus had appointed Judas Iscariot as one of the original twelve apostles (Matthew 10:1–4). After Judas's betrayal and death, Peter led the other believers in choosing a successor, in accordance with prophecies concerning Judas found in Psalm 109:8.

4. James Douglas Grant Dunn, *Jesus and the Spirit: A Study of the Religious and Charismatic Experience of Jesus and the First Christians as Reflected in the New Testament* (Philadelphia: The Westminster Press, 1975), 282.

5. Ibid., 289.

6. David Johannes du Plessis, *The Spirit Bade Me Go* (Plainfield, NJ: Logos International, 1977), 15.

Chapter 5

MANIFESTATIONS OF THE HOLY SPIRIT

FIRST CORINTHIANS 12 begins, *"Now about spiritual [matters], brothers, I do not want you to be ignorant"* (v. 1).[1] With these words, the apostle Paul opened his three-chapter discourse concerning the Holy Spirit's operation among gathered Christians. Frequently, English versions of the Bible translate the opening phrase in this way: "Now, about spiritual gifts...." Nevertheless, the word *gifts* cannot be found in the original text.

THE APOSTLE PAUL AND "SPIRITUALS"

Paul used the Greek word *pneumatikon*, which literally means "spirituals." The word is derived from *pneuma*, meaning "spirit," "breath," or "wind." In 1526, Bible translator and reformer William Tyndale translated the concept accurately as "spiritual things."[2] Paul used *pneumatikon* in a distinctive way to describe the action of God. This word clearly conveys the concept of being possessed by the Spirit, embodying the Spirit, and making the Spirit

61

visible. The subject it describes relates to the essence, or nature, of the Spirit.[3]

Certainly, the "spiritual things" about which Paul wrote are gifts. All of God's dealings with humanity originate from His unconditional love for His creation. The apostle did not intend for us to see the things of the Spirit as objects we own, to use or abuse at our own discretion. God imparts gifts of the Holy Spirit to us as believers so that we will come closer to Christ. We belong to the Lord!

In 1 Corinthians 12:4, Paul uniquely introduced another term into the Christian vocabulary. He wrote, *"There are different kinds of gifts."* The word translated as *"gifts," charismata,* is a word with which we are already familiar from its singular form, *charisma.* However, this word does not simply mean "talented" or "gifted," as contemporary secular usage of the word would imply, but it further describes the exploits associated with the Holy Spirit. The root of *charismata* is *charis,* meaning "grace"—God's unmerited favor. The source of these exploits is in God's grace. Not surprisingly, we discover that *charis* is also related to *chara,* the word for "joy." When one is in communion with the Holy Spirit and God's people, there is an abiding joy.

"There are different kinds of gifts, but the same Spirit" (v. 4). When a believer is baptized in the Holy Spirit, he receives the gift of the Holy Spirit. Because of this, when we surrender to the Spirit, He may manifest Himself through whatever gifts, or extensions of grace, He chooses.

The Holy Spirit is "God Himself close to man and the world, as comprehending but not comprehensible, the bestowing but not controllable, the life-creating but also judging power and force."[4] How does God show Himself to us? The Holy Spirit unveils Himself when operating through God's people.

As Paul wrote of spiritual things, he contrasted those of divine origin with those generated by demonic activity. *"No one who is speaking by the Spirit of God says, 'Jesus be cursed,' and no one can say, 'Jesus is Lord,' except by the Holy Spirit"* (v. 3). When one comes under the influence of God's Spirit, that person always affirms God's message: Jesus is Lord. Any other source does not attest to this truth.

Some suggest that *"speaking by the Spirit of God"* refers to speaking in tongues. Others assume it includes prophetic utterance as well. Paul's message is this: When people surrender to God's power, they do not need to fear that they will blaspheme God, as some assert. Jesus taught:

> *Which of you, if his son asks for bread, will give him a stone? Or if he asks for a fish, will give him a snake? If you, then, though you are evil, know how to give good gifts to your children, how much more will your Father in heaven give good gifts to those who ask him!*
> *(Matthew 7:9–11)*

GIFTS ARE FOR THE COMMON GOOD

Paul instructed, *"Now to each one the manifestation of the Spirit is given for the common good"* (1

Corinthians 12:7). Here Paul used the word *"manifestation"* to describe all of the various under-takings of the Spirit. Biblical scholar Howard Ervin writes:

> By their very nature, the manifestations of the Spirit...are not private gifts to be exercised by the *gifted* [Ervin's emphasis] at their will or whim. They are designed by the Spirit to minister to present needs in the community of believers.[5]

In the list of the manifestations of the Spirit in 1 Corinthians 12:8–10, Paul included these gifts: the message of wisdom, the message of knowledge (translated as word of wisdom and word of knowledge in the King James Version), faith, gifts of healing, miraculous powers, prophetic utterance, the ability to distinguish between spirits, speaking in tongues, and interpretation of tongues. God confers these disclosures of the Holy Spirit's presence to the church to uplift her. Those through whom God operates to bring these gifts to the church are God's agents, servants, and conduits. Therefore, when God uses us to bring a manifestation of the Spirit, we are instrumental in conveying a blessing to His people.

Often, a Christian believer will say, "I do not know what my spiritual gift is. On occasion, God has used me in bringing a prophecy. At other times, the Lord has led me to pray for someone's healing. Am I a prophet or a healer?" This person misunderstands the nature of the manifestations of the Spirit. Yes, God allots each of us a unique ministry and prepares us in numerous ways, but the Holy Spirit manifests Himself as He wills, in different ways at various times.

One fact is clear as we read 1 Corinthians 12–14: God wants to employ each believer. No one is to be an observer. God makes available to every follower of Christ the assortment of manifestations of the Holy Spirit. Every manifestation of the Spirit has a purpose and is useful.

Paul characterized the distribution and diversity of the Spirit's action among God's people.[6] He wrote, *"There are different kinds of service, but the same Lord"* (1 Corinthians 12:5). Here we find the word *diakoniai*, "acts of service," related to the words *deacon* and *servant*. We can translate this passage as "differences of ministries." Each of us has a unique role in God's plan. As we follow God's direction, manifestations of the Spirit enable us to fulfill the distinct mission to which He has called us.

Paul proceeded, *"There are different kinds of working, but the same God works all of them in all men"* (v. 6). The word he used in this verse for "workings," *energemata*, is the basis for our word *energy*. It is God's power alone that enables us to manifest the gifts. No matter what the manifestation is, the credit goes to God, the source of these workings.

All these gifts of God's grace, acts of service, and divine activities are manifestations of God's Spirit. From the context, we might construct a more helpful interpretation of Paul's opening phrase in 1 Corinthians 12:1: *"Now about spiritual* [manifestations]...." Howard Ervin writes, "The translation 'spiritual *manifestations'* [Ervin's emphasis] satisfies the criteria of grammar, syntax, and context...."[7] We must never forget the role of God's sovereignty in all of this, for the apostle also wrote, *"All these are the work of one and the same Spirit, and he gives them to each one, just as he determines"* (v. 11).

CATEGORIES OF SPIRITUAL MANIFESTATIONS

The Lord provides every manifestation of His Spirit for a distinct need that should be addressed. These demonstrations of God's power among us fall into some basic categories that the apostle Paul has outlined for us.

There are three groups within Paul's list of spiritual manifestations in the passage we have just been examining. First, Paul described the gifts of revelation. Among these are the word of wisdom, the word of knowledge, and the distinguishing of spirits. Secondly, Paul outlined manifestations that display God's power. These demonstration gifts include faith, the working of miracles, and gifts of healing. Thirdly, Paul specified the communication gifts: prophecy, speaking in tongues, and the interpretation of tongues.

You may ask, "Does the Bible say that any of the manifestations of the Holy Spirit would disappear at the end of the apostolic age?" No, it does not. Nowhere does Scripture say that any of these manifestations will cease to exist during the church age. Paul did write, *"Where there are prophecies, they will cease; where there are tongues, they will be stilled;*

where there is knowledge, it will pass away" (1 Corinthians 13:8). However, he went on to say that this will not happen until *"perfection"* (v. 10) has come. The most straightforward interpretation of this passage, considering the context, is that these things will disappear when Jesus returns.[8] Therefore, the Scriptures teach the perpetuity of the spiritual gifts.

A Variety of Manifestations of the Spirit

Many speak about the "nine gifts of the Spirit" because nine gifts are listed in 1 Corinthians 12. You may be asking yourself, "Does God constrain Himself to only nine gifts of the Spirit?" Of course, God does not. The apostle Paul wrote 1 Corinthians to a particular church with particular needs; in an earlier part of this letter, we see that the congregation had written him for answers to several problems. Paul listed nine kinds of specific manifestations of the Holy Spirit to help them understand the variety of the Spirit's manifestations. As we make ourselves available to the Lord's guidance, we find Him disclosing Himself to us and through us in an unlimited number of ways.

Because we have surrendered to the Lord, we belong to Him (1 Corinthians 6:19–20), and He endues—or, clothes—us with power. When God manifests His Spirit through us, we are His representatives, but He is in control. It is not our job to operate God's gifts. Instead, we surrender to God and watch Him work through us to accomplish His purposes.

We should never fall into the trap of believing that we must exactly duplicate every pattern in the early church. Paul gave us a list of spiritual manifestations, but they are, in a sense, broad categories. Often, manifestations of the Spirit are difficult to classify. Let me tell you about an unusual manifestation of the Spirit that took place a number of years ago.

I was in a service in West Virginia where my father-in-law was pastoring. In this service I was spiritually, emotionally, and physically overcome by the Holy Spirit; many people call this being "slain in the Spirit." The phenomenon of being overcome by the Spirit—an experience that Paul had, as recorded in Acts 9:4, 26:14, and 2 Corinthians 12:2, and that John had, as recorded in Revelation 1:10—seems to accompany every great Protestant revival movement.

In his *Journal*, John Wesley tells of some who, during his preaching, "were struck to the ground." Other historic revival leaders who experienced the phenomenon of people "falling out in the Spirit" include Jonathan Edwards, George Whitefield, and Methodist circuit rider Peter Cartwright.[9] It is not unusual for people to experience this heavenly occurrence in the current Pentecostal revival that is sweeping the globe.[10]

I was lost in the Spirit for several hours. While I was in this spiritual state, God showed me the world, my ministry, and what I was to accomplish. He revealed to me where I was to minister through the years. He displayed to me where He would take me, from one sphere, one level, one plateau to another in my ministry.

During that service, the Holy Spirit moved upon me, and I began to point out individuals in the congregation. I was under the anointing, guided by the Spirit. As I would point out people, they would run to the altar and give their hearts to Christ or be filled with the Spirit.

One man was living quite a loose life as far as his commitment to God was concerned. As the power of God began to move, he got up and went out of the service. Although my eyes were closed and I was in the Spirit, my finger went right to him and followed him as he walked out of the church. He stayed out of the church for a while. Then as he came back into the building, my finger again pointed toward him and followed him until he sat down. This unusual manifestation of God's presence visibly moved him, and he began to weep. He worked in a coal mine, and after the service he went to work. Sometime after midnight, he was killed. He was riding on a battery-operated coal cart when the accident occurred. His head was crushed, and he died immediately. I believe God gave him a supernatural warning that night. I don't know if he got things right with God, but the Lord gave him the opportunity to do so.

While Paul never explicitly mentioned "the pointing of a finger" as a manifestation of the Spirit, in this incident it clearly was. Do not expect God's actions always to fit nicely into our preconceived notions.

Notes

1. The *New International Version* translates this verse using the words "spiritual gifts" rather than "spiritual matters." It follows some earlier English versions in doing so. As we continue this study, we will discover why the translation of this term can cause confusion. Also, when the Greek text uses the plural word for "brothers," it may also be translated to refer to both genders: "brothers and sisters."

2. Howard Matthew Ervin, *Spirit Baptism: A Biblical Investigation* (Peabody, MA: Hendrickson Publishers, 1987), 86.

3. James Douglas Grant Dunn, *Jesus and the Spirit: A Study of the Religious and Charismatic Experience of Jesus and the First Christians as Reflected in the New Testament* (Philadelphia: The Westminster Press, 1975), 207–208.

4. Hans Küng, *Does God Exist?: An Answer for Today,* trans. Edward Quinn (Garden City, NY: Doubleday, 1980), 696.

5. Ervin, *Spirit Baptism,* 92.

6. Dunn, *Jesus and the Spirit,* 209.

7. Ervin, *Spirit Baptism,* 96.

8. Ibid., 174–176.

9. Patrick H. Alexander, "Slain in the Spirit," in *Dictionary of Pentecostal and Charismatic Movements,* ed. Stanley M. Burgess, Gary B. McGee, and Patrick H. Alexander (Grand Rapids, MI: Zondervan Publishing House, 1988), 789–791.

10. For a more complete discussion of this experience, see Alexander, "Slain in the Spirit."

Chapter 6

REVELATION GIFTS

ONE MARVELOUS ASPECT of the Christian life is that God still speaks to His people. If you do all the talking during times of prayer, you miss what God wants to say to you. Just as we share secrets with those closest to us, God shares His plans with us: *"Surely the Sovereign LORD does nothing without revealing his plan to his servants the prophets"* (Amos 3:7). From a natural standpoint, we depend on our five senses: sight, hearing, smell, taste, and touch. When we enter the fullness of the Holy Spirit, we find God revealing information to us through our spirits.

In our study of Paul's catalog of spiritual manifestations from 1 Corinthians 12, we observed that he began by listing the word of wisdom and the word of knowledge. Later in the list, he mentioned a manifestation that helps us to distinguish spirits. These are all "God-given disclosures" that "reveal the things of God to whom He indwells."[1] Although Scripture only briefly mentions these manifestations, we find that they occupy quite useful places in our daily Christian experience.

71

In Isaiah 11:2, we read a prophecy that the Spirit of the Lord will rest on the Messiah. This prophecy identifies the Holy Spirit as *"the Spirit of wisdom and of understanding, the Spirit of counsel and of power, the Spirit of knowledge and of the fear of the LORD."* As the Spirit envelops us, empowering us for Christian service, we find these attributes exhibited in the manifestations of the Spirit.

The sharing of significant information cements close, personal relationships. Military forces win wars when generals and soldiers effectively communicate. Similarly, Christians need information from God. When Paul summarized the manifestations of the Holy Spirit, he included this important area in the Christian life: hearing directly from God.

WORD OF WISDOM AND WORD OF KNOWLEDGE

While the idea of knowing God and receiving divinely given wisdom is found throughout the Scriptures, the specific reference to *"the word of wisdom"* and *"the word of knowledge"* is found only in 1 Corinthians 12:8 (KJV). These two manifestations work closely together. It is significant that Paul used the term *"word."*

We can also translate the Greek term *logos,* which Paul employed here, as "message," "matter," or "concern." We do not have to confine its meaning to a spoken word.[2] The expression implies information and instructions given for a specific situation. If someone receives a word of wisdom or a word of knowledge, that person becomes neither a database of all knowledge nor the source of infinite wisdom. Some things remain God's secrets (Deuteronomy 29:29). God alone is all-knowing, and He is the well of wisdom that never runs dry.[3]

If God gives you a word about someone, that does not mean that you know everything about that individual. You cannot read that person's mind. Those who are involved in espionage are given information by their governments on a need-to-know basis. Knowing too much could compromise a mission and, at times, endanger the agent. As you experience God working through you, you will discover that the Holy Spirit tells you only what you need to know. With this gift, God is reaching out to others through us so that we may aid in this area of God's blessing. It is exciting to know that He will also reach out to us through others to let us know that He knows everything about us as well.

A word of caution is needed here. While these supernatural manifestations of the Holy Spirit bring us knowledge we could never have otherwise, they must never be confused with things from the world of the occult. God expressly forbids any involvement with psychic activity, divination, sorcery, clairvoyance, witchcraft, interpreting omens, contacting the dead, and mind reading (Deuteronomy 18:9–12). In the biblical account of King Saul's death, we see that God judged him for consulting a medium for guidance (1 Chronicles 10:13).

How does the Bible define wisdom? The Greek word Paul used in 1 Corinthians 12:8 is *sophia*, which was understood by the early church as the approach one takes toward life.[4] The early Christians perceived wisdom as something that comes from God. The Greek word Paul used for knowledge is *gnosis*, which usually means "that which we notice, experience, or observe."[5] It refers to the close relationship with God we have as Christians. It could also include cognitive perception of facts.

It will be helpful to first take a look at the word of knowledge. This manifestation of God's Spirit conveys information from God that does not come from natural sources. It is God disclosing specific insights concerning physical, emotional, psychological, and spiritual problems.[6] It deals with facts.

On the other hand, a word of wisdom deals with reasons.[7] Such a word guides us in using the knowledge that God imparts to us. This wisdom also helps us to deal with situations and to integrate other manifestations of the Spirit effectively. It can free us from traps set by God's enemies and help us respond to interrogation during times of persecution. (See Matthew 10:19–20; Luke 21:15.)[8]

We may verbally share these words of wisdom or words of knowledge with others, although not always. In some cases, God bestows on us the insight to act appropriately but prevents us from divulging to anyone else what He has revealed to us.

King Solomon highly valued wisdom. When God promised him that he could have whatever he desired, this monarch asked for *"a discerning heart"* (1 Kings 3:9), for *"wisdom"* and *"knowledge"* (2 Chronicles 1:10) to guide his actions and illuminate his understanding of right and wrong. From Proverbs 1:7, we learn that *"the fear of the LORD is the beginning of knowledge, but fools despise wisdom and discipline."* Paul made it apparent that wisdom from God far surpasses human wisdom (1 Corinthians 2:4–7). James 1:5 advises us that we can ask for wisdom: *"If any of you lacks wisdom, he should ask God, who gives generously to all without finding fault, and it will be given to him."*

It is significant that Paul listed the word of wisdom first when he described the manifestations of the Spirit in 1 Corinthians 12. We need God's wisdom to wisely employ any gift. We need to approach every situation carefully according to God's plan. A word of wisdom will lead us in the right direction. Such situations demand "proper judgment for action."[9] You may own a highly advanced computer, but if you don't know how to turn it on and use it, it's simply a very expensive box. The same correlation applies to a word of wisdom and a word of knowledge. To fully implement a word of knowledge, we require a word of wisdom.

Some imagine that you have to be a recluse in a far-off monastery to hear a word from God. Others think hours of meditation will bring an answer. On the pages of the New Testament, we find a group of people who were constantly hearing from God. It should not be any different for Christians today. God wants a relationship with humankind and will reveal His plan to those who seek Him.

We notice in the Scriptures that when Jesus lived on earth, He sought the Father in prayer. He spent the entire night in prayer before He selected His twelve disciples (Luke 6:12–13). Jesus also had insight into the lives of people He had never met before. (See John 1:48; 4:17–18; Luke 19:5.)

Jesus once asked His closest disciples, *"Who do people say the Son of Man is?"* (Matthew 16:13). His followers listed many possibilities that they had heard outsiders propose, including the idea that He was John the Baptist, Elijah, or Jeremiah. Then Jesus inquired of them, *"Who do you say I am?"* (v. 15). Peter recognized Jesus as the Messiah, the Son of the living God. Jesus explained that only the heavenly Father could have revealed such knowledge; it could not have come from natural perception.

In the book of Acts, we observe that God revealed things to His people constantly. For instance, God showed Peter the deception of Ananias and Sapphira. (See Acts 5:1–11.) God also prepared Peter to meet the Roman military officer Cornelius and to lead him into the fullness of God's grace. (See Acts 10:1–48.) In Damascus, God prepared another disciple named Ananias to minister to a new convert. It was Saul of Tarsus who became Paul, the great apostle to the nations. (See Acts 9:10–19.)

Unlike more spectacular demonstrations of God's power, such as healings and speaking in tongues, revelations from God often come quietly. We must be careful not to miss them. We do not have to act strangely to manifest God's Spirit. God wants us to be normal, but to be "supernaturally natural."[10] At times, God provides us with the right word to say or helps us to handle a situation in a certain manner, and we do not even realize we have experienced a manifestation of the Spirit.

Ministers often rely on God's words of wisdom to solve difficult circumstances. However, God does not give words of knowledge and wisdom only to the "professional" clergy. While one believer is encouraging another, a word may be spoken that both recognize has come from God. It is a message that brings a sense of peace to a troubling situation.

Often, in meetings where the Spirit is moving, the church will receive, through various members, words of knowledge concerning certain problems. These may include diseases, afflictions, financial worries, and family problems. God dispenses such words to those in need so they may obtain the relief the Lord wants to bring them. Through the years, God has used such messages to strengthen people's faith and to answer their prayers in ways that further glorify Him.

DISCERNING OF SPIRITS

We often experience another manifestation of the Spirit that we find easy to ignore: the discerning of spirits. We may feel "funny"; things might not seem right to us. Yet we may fail to recognize that this feeling is God showing us that something is in fact wrong. God equips us with the ability to discern between spirits, to discover what is from God and what is not.

Regarding the gift of discerning of spirits, Michael Green writes, "There are few gifts more necessary to the church."[11] The apostle John warned, *"Test the spirits to see whether they are from God, because many false prophets have gone out into the world"* (1 John 4:1). John continued by supplying guidelines for detecting false teaching. Congregations are to test supposed words from God (1 Corinthians 14:29). Jesus taught that bad trees will become evident because they will bear bad fruit (Matthew 7:15–20).

Modern man falls short of acknowledging the reality of spiritual beings. Yet, the Holy Spirit and God's angels, as well as Satan and his demons, are all around us. Failing to identify the surrounding spirits makes us ineffective in dealing with spiritual problems. Christians are fighting spiritual battles, continually receiving attacks from Satan and his forces. In these battles, we must remember something extremely significant: the powers of good and evil are not equal. There are not two gods—one good and one bad. Scripture clarifies this distinction. God is infinitely greater than the Devil: *"The one who is in you is greater than the one who is in the world"* (1 John 4:4).

When we become aware of the spiritual nature of the world in which we live, the need for discerning spirits becomes readily apparent. Heribert Mühlen writes, "The gift of discernment and testing results in a *judgment*" (Mühlen's emphasis).[12] This ability assists us in classifying the spiritual source of something, such as a manifestation, a teaching, a prophecy, or a sickness. There are three types of spiritual domains that we need to identify.

The Domain of God

First, there is God's domain. This includes His Spirit, along with His angels, who are God's messengers and servants. If something is from God, we should accept it as such. Yet everything that comes our way is not necessarily from God, although He may allow it into our lives.

The Domain of Satan

Secondly, there are evil spirits. It is obvious that not every spiritual manifestation is from God. Unfortunately, demons do not always identify themselves. They refuse to wear the appropriate costumes. Rarely do they come with horns and pitchforks. Satan himself comes *"as an angel of light"* (2 Corinthians 11:14). He is beautiful to behold. He makes evil attractive, and he distorts truth. One of his names is the Father of Lies (John 8:44). The Devil yearns to be worshipped, despite the fact that worship belongs to God alone. Demonic spirits do Satan's bidding and specialize in temptation, deception, sickness, and disaster.

The enemy of God is *"the spirit of the antichrist"* (1 John 4:3), the counterfeit or substitute messiah (2:18–19). Scripture warns us to beware of false prophets and messiahs (Matthew 24:4–5). Not everyone who calls Jesus *"Lord, Lord"* (7:21) truly follows Christ.

We may encounter those whom evil spirits have possessed. In my ministry, I have confronted many incidences of demon possession. Demonized people need deliverance. In the Scriptures, we read that one woman acclaimed Paul and his companions in ministry as *"servants of the Most High God"* (Acts 16:17), but Paul was not flattered. God enabled him to distinguish between spirits. Paul recognized that a devil possessed this woman, and he cast it out (v. 18). God also has used me in bringing deliverance to many tortured individuals.

All believers have authority over the Devil. Jesus said that believers would cast out devils in His name. Don't go looking for trouble, seeing demons behind every bush or under every rock. But if you come upon a demon-possessed person, you can do something. As a Spirit-filled Christian, you have the power to rescue that individual from evil by God's help. We will take a closer look at this area as we study the working of miracles in a later chapter.

Remember that Satan is master of the counterfeit. He seeks to deceive and mislead people with his own signs and wonders. Fortunately, as we stay in tune with God, He will aid us in knowing the difference between His works and Satan's works.

The Domain of the Human Spirit

Finally, we will encounter the human spirit: the spirits of men and women. The Bible tells us that man is a spiritual being. The human spirit is what defines us as people. It is the self, the mind, that "aspect of the personality...which is capable of responding to the divine."[13] In Genesis 2:7, we find that God gave man life by breathing into him. When the human spirit is revitalized by salvation and the presence of the Holy Spirit, and is submitted to Christ's lordship, it wonderfully reflects the image of God received in Creation.

Sadly, when people are unsaved, their human spirits rebel against their Creator. Because of their sin, they are separated from fellowship with God and are spiritually dead. Their sinful human natures easily give in to temptation. Their lack of recognition of God's authority leads them astray.

Christians can also be deceived by their own spirits, or the spirits of others, when they lack faith in God or permit their selfish sinful natures to rule in their lives. Especially during times when we are not living closely to God, we may mistake our human spirits for God's voice. At other times, our own desires may be so strong that we block out what God is saying, preferring to follow our own yearnings. This self-deception can be disastrous. Our only protection against it is to constantly surrender our wills to God.

Being influenced by weak and sinful human nature or demonic deception often leads to error in both belief and practice. For this reason, believers must desire spiritual discernment, working hand-in-hand with the word of knowledge and the word of wisdom. It is necessary to know who or what is behind the situations we face. God has given us these manifestations of divine revelation to enable us to do this.

These manifestations have aided me many times in dealing with a variety of situations. Rarely would I commence to solve people's problems without asking God to help me discern the spirits involved in the particular circumstance. Through the word of knowledge and the word of wisdom, God enables me to minister effectively, and He will do the same for any believer.

Notes

1. Edward Michael Bankers Green, *I Believe in the Holy Spirit* (Grand Rapids, MI: William B. Eerdmans Publishing Company, 1975), 181.

2. Dennis Joseph Bennett and Rita Bennett, *The Holy Spirit and You: A Study Guide to the Spirit-Filled Life* (Plainfield, NJ: Logos International, 1971), 156.

3. B. E. Underwood, *The Gifts of the Spirit: Supernatural Equipment for Christian Service* (Franklin Springs, GA: Advocate Press, 1967), 29.

4. J. Goetzman, "Wisdom: Sophia," in *The New International Dictionary of New Testament Theology (NIDNTT)*, ed. Colin Brown (Grand Rapids, MI: Zondervan Publishing House, 1978), 3:1030.

5. E. D. Schmitz, "Knowledge: Ginosko," *NIDNTT*, 2:394.

6. Charles H. Kraft, *Christianity with Power: Your Worldview and Your Experience of the Supernatural* (Ann Arbor, MI: Vine Books, 1989), 52.

7. Underwood, *The Gifts of the Spirit*, 29.

8. Cecil M. Robeck, Jr., "Word of Wisdom," in *Dictionary of Pentecostal and Charismatic Movements*, ed. Stanley M. Burgess, Gary B. McGee, and Patrick H. Alexander (Grand Rapids, MI: Zondervan Publishing House, 1988), 892.

9. Bennett and Bennett, *The Holy Spirit and You*, 155.

10. David du Plessis is given credit for this expression in Larry Christenson's book *Speaking in Tongues and Its Significance for the Church* (Minneapolis, MN: Dimension Books, 1968), 120.

11. Green, *I Believe in the Holy Spirit*, 188, 192.

12. Heribert Mühlen, *A Charismatic Theology: Initiation in the Spirit* (New York: Paulist Press, 1978), 176.

13. Charles Francis Digby Moule, *The Holy Spirit* (Grand Rapids, MI: William B. Eerdmans Publishing Company, 1978), 17.

Chapter 7

THE GIFT OF FAITH

L ET US CLOSELY examine the manifestation of faith that the apostle Paul listed in his "charismatic manifesto" (1 Corinthians 12–14). In doing so, we must also look at the various related concepts of faith in the New Testament. The Greek word in 1 Corinthians 12:9 that we translate as *"faith," pistis*, means "to trust, depend, and rely on." In Hebrews 11:6, we learn that *"without faith it is impossible to please God, because anyone who comes to him must believe that he exists and that he rewards those who earnestly seek him."* Faith is essential to the Christian life.

THE BIBLICAL CONCEPT OF FAITH

Biblical faith is much more than knowing about God or simply believing in God's existence. The Bible tells us that *"even the demons believe that—and shudder"* (James 2:19). While intellectual acknowledgment of a Supreme Being is a starting point, a further element is indispensable. We must put our trust in this God. The writer of Hebrews gives us a definition of biblical faith: *"Now faith is being sure of what we hope for and certain of what we do not see"* (Hebrews 11:1). We must be willing to believe God and His promises to the point of risking the resulting consequences to obey Him, assured that He will keep His pledge to us.[1]

Every Christian, by definition, has saving faith, the faith that saves a person from sin and judgment and makes him a new creature in Christ. Through God's grace, we can respond to His offer of salvation by trusting Christ, yet God never violates our free wills. We have the choice to accept or reject God's invitation. Every man and woman must face the crossroads that will decide his or her eternal destiny.

Saving faith helps us to understand that *"in the beginning was the Word, and the Word was with God, and the Word was God"* (John 1:1). This same Word, whom we know as Jesus, pitched His tent, His tabernacle, among men and women. The Word became a human being (v. 14). Saving faith acknowledges Jesus as the Lamb of God who takes away our sin. When He hung on the cross, He paid the penalty for our sins in our stead. Justifying faith enables us to say, *"Jesus is Lord"* (Romans 10:9) and to believe in our hearts that God raised Him from the dead (v. 9).

Saving faith comes to us by hearing God's Word: *"Faith comes from hearing the message, and the message is heard through the word of Christ"* (v. 17). Moses once explained that God does not make unreasonable demands that only supermen and superwomen can fulfill. *"No,"* he said, *"the word is very near you; it is in your mouth and in your heart so you may obey it"* (Deuteronomy 30:14). Paul quoted this passage in Romans 10:8 to explain how the word of faith, in other words, the Gospel of Christ, is accessible to all who will believe: *"'The word is near you; it is in your mouth and in your heart,' that is, the word of faith we are proclaiming."*

Paul also talked about each of us having a *"measure of faith"*: *"Do not think of yourself more highly than you ought, but rather think of yourself with sober judgment, in accordance with the measure of faith God has given you"* (Romans 12:3). Paul went on to write how our roles in God's plan depend on the measure, or proportion, of faith that God gives us to fulfill His plan. God will provide the faith we need to perform the assignment for which He has prepared us.

FALSE FAITH

Never confuse biblical faith with occultic and New Age concepts. Faith is not an impersonal force, as many non-Christian cults teach. It is utter dependence on an all-powerful God, not a substance out of which God made the universe. Unlike witchcraft, which uses particular formulas in an attempt to manipulate the laws of the spirit world, faith surrenders to God's plan and direction for our lives.

The book of James tells us that a tongue can be both a tool of blessing and a tool of destruction (3:9). God will hold us accountable for every idle word we speak (Matthew 12:36). We need to watch what we say. A constant reinforcement of negative statements can actually lead to self-fulfilling prophecies. The words we use are important; speak words of faith in agreement with what God has said in His Word. It is not our speaking of the words that is important, but the fact that God has made a promise is important, indeed. God is in control, not man. As you exercise your faith, avoid anything that is occultic in nature. Always keep focused on God and His promises. The Bible impels us to place our trust in God, not in our faith.

Genuine faith will never permit us to approach God with arrogance. Faith causes us to humble ourselves before our Creator. A popular gospel song expresses faith well: "God said it. I believe it. That settles it for me."

SUFFICIENT FAITH

We read in the Bible that in some situations, Jesus rebuked people for their lack of faith. In other incidents, He commended individuals for their great faith. Yet insufficient faith is only one of many reasons why God may not answer our prayers as we want Him to. Sometimes God's answers are no. The Scriptures say that God will not answer our prayers if we waver doubtfully when we ask or if we pray selfishly (James 1:6–7; 4:3). God's timing also plays a part in determining when prayers are answered (Romans 1:10).

God often places obstacles in our lives for a purpose. We try to run from them, but they show up again. Paul asked God three times to remove his *"thorn in* [the] *flesh"* (2 Corinthians 12:7). We do not know exactly what that *"thorn"* was. Some people think it was an illness. Others believe it was a person who claimed to have more spiritual authority than Paul. Some commentators believe the thorn was literally a *"messenger of Satan"* (v. 7), a demonic spirit. Whatever it was, God refused to take it away because He had allowed it there to keep Paul humble. God told Paul, *"My grace is sufficient for you, for my power is made perfect in weakness"* (v. 9).

When making some requests, we can be confident that God will answer our prayers. When God has granted a promise in His Word, the Bible, we know it is His will:

> *This is the confidence we have in approaching God: that if we ask anything according to his will, he hears us. And if we know that he hears us—whatever we ask—we know that we have what we asked of him.*　　*(1 John 5:14–15)*

If we ask God to save us, we know He will. *"Everyone who calls on the name of the Lord will be saved"* (Acts 2:21, quoting Joel 2:32). If we ask the Lord to fill us with His Holy Spirit, we know He will. *"Be filled with the Spirit"* (Ephesians 5:18). If we ask the Almighty to provide for our needs, we can be certain that He will take care of us. *"My God will meet all your needs according to his glorious riches in Christ Jesus"* (Philippians 4:19).

As Oral Roberts frequently used to say, when explaining why he confidently prayed that God would bless people, "God is a good God!" *"Taste and see that the LORD is good"* (Psalm 34:8). Jesus is our healer! *"He took up our infirmities and carried our diseases"* (Matthew 8:17, quoting Isaiah 53:4). Our heavenly Father will deliver us from all evil. *"I will fear no evil, for you are with me; your rod and your staff, they comfort me"* (Psalm 23:4). We can pray for God to save our families. *"Believe in the Lord Jesus, and you will be saved—you and your household"* (Acts 16:31). These are all examples of how we can exercise confident and expectant faith in God, trusting Him to answer in His perfect will and way, in fulfillment of His perfect plan.

THE MANIFESTATION OF FAITH

However, after reviewing the biblical under-standing of faith, we must still ask: What is this par-ticular manifestation of faith to which Paul refers in 1 Corinthians 12? Some define the manifestation of faith as "a sudden surge of faith...without doubt."[2] There are times, often in a crisis, when the Spirit enables us to believe confidently that as we act or speak in Jesus' name, God will mightily respond on our behalf.

Jesus referred to this kind of faith when He said,

> *I tell you the truth, if anyone says to this mountain, "Go, throw yourself into the sea,"*

and does not doubt in his heart but believes that what he says will happen, it will be done for him. *(Mark 11:23)*

He also said, *"If you have faith as small as a mustard seed,...nothing will be impossible for you"* (Matthew 17:20).

It was a manifestation of faith that enabled Peter to address the crowd on the Day of Pentecost and to explain the unusual phenomenon of the outpouring of the Holy Spirit. (See Acts 2:1–41.) This same gift was in operation when Peter and John encountered the lame man begging near the temple. (See Acts 3:1–8.) Instead of meeting this beggar's temporal needs, God gave Peter and John the boldness to say, *"Silver or gold I do not have, but what I have I give you. In the name of Jesus Christ of Nazareth, walk"* (v. 6). When the man was healed, he began to praise God, and this led others to do the same (vv. 9–10).

This gift not only operates to bring about healings and miracles, but it also empowers believers to face persecution. In Daniel 3, a manifestation of faith helped the Old Testament saints Shadrach, Meshach, and Abednego to face entering the fiery furnace rather than engage in idolatry.[3] Surely the gift of faith strengthened the apostles to continue proclaiming Jesus after the rulers, elders, and teachers of the law in Jerusalem warned them not to do so. (See Acts 4:1–20.) This manifestation has enabled many believers to meet death without wavering. As Stephen was stoned to death, he prayed with faith, *"Lord, do not hold this sin against them"* (Acts 7:60).

God-given courage was surely at work in the life of Polycarp, a disciple of the apostle John and an early Christian martyr. Church history records the brave execution of this second-generation Christian who refused to deny Christ. Theologian and church historian Eusebius (*c.* 260–*c.* 340), in his *Ecclesiastical History,* quotes Polycarp as saying to the Romans, "Eighty and six years have I served Him [Christ], and He never did me wrong; and how can I now blaspheme my King that has saved me?" Despite threats of death through horrible methods, tradition records that Polycarp "was filled with confidence and joy, and his countenance was brightened with grace." As he was being prepared to be burned alive, he said, "For He that gives me strength to bear the fire, will also give me power without being secured by you with these spikes, to remain unmoved on the pile." After this, his captors did not nail him, but "merely bound him to the stake." As the flames were leaping around his body, he continued to give glory to God.[4]

Each of us, as we follow Jesus, will face trials and difficulties. As we trust God, our loving Lord will provide the faith we need to meet any situation. Faith, gifts of healing, and the working of miracles labor closely together, as we will see in our continuing study of the manifestations of the Spirit.

FAITH AND A MIRACLE IN HONDURAS

A manifestation of faith played a part in a powerful miracle that took place in the country of Honduras. I was conducting meetings at a city auditorium that seated several thousand people. On the first night I preached a short message about faith and trust in God. The Holy Spirit instructed me to minister to the sick. I called for all of the people in the congregation who wanted prayer for healing. Men, women, boys, and girls lined up all the way around the huge auditorium.

While they were gathering for prayer, the Holy Spirit spoke to me and said, "God is going to heal the first five people in this prayer line tonight." This was, of course, a word of knowledge. God was telling me what He was going to do. Nevertheless, a gift of faith would also be required to enable God's promise to come to pass, as you will soon see.

I began to pray for the sick. I asked the first man standing in the line what his problem was. He did not answer. A gentleman standing close to him said, "This man is totally deaf and mute." I came to the second man and I said, "What is your problem?" The same man on the side answered for him as well, saying, "He is also deaf and mute." I came to the third person and asked, "What is your problem?" The same man on the side replied, "He is deaf and mute." By the time I came to the fourth person, I turned to the man on the side and said, "And is he deaf and mute?" The man answered, "Yes." The fifth man was also deaf and mute. All five could neither hear nor talk.

I had a promise from God that He was going to heal the first five people for whom I would pray. Remember, none of them could hear or speak. The

Devil jumped on my shoulder and jeered, "You have really played the fool now. If your God does not heal these people, you're going to look like a fool, and you will have to pack your bags and go back to America." I responded, "Yes, Devil. But when God does heal them, you're going to look like a fool, and you're going to have to pack your bags and get out of town. If God said it, He will do it. You can depend on God to do what He promises."

God gave me the faith to pray for these five individuals. I laid my hands on the first man and took authority over that foul deaf and dumb spirit in the power and the name of Jesus, commanding it to loose the man, come out of him, and never return to him again. When I had finished addressing the demon, I felt the Holy Spirit surge through my body, and I knew that God had performed a miracle.

At this point, I got close to the man and said two words, "Say, 'Hallelujah.'" When I uttered those words, the man flinched. He was hearing for the first time in his life. He smiled and said, "Hallelujah!" I don't mean that he spoke in baby talk or unintelligible language; he said "Hallelujah" as clearly and distinctly as I can say it. I came to the second man. Before I could pray for him, he said, "Hallelujah!" The third man said, "Hallelujah!" The fourth man said, "Hallelujah!" The fifth man said, "Hallelujah!" The power of God had healed all of them simultaneously. I want to tell you, I also shouted, "Hallelujah!" and rejoiced in the power of God's deliverance.

After those five healings, I closed the service. I did not pray for anyone else that night. When we arrived at the auditorium the following night, people had filled the building to capacity. Outside, there were perhaps enough people to fill another building. The atmosphere was charged with faith. On that night, I preached a short salvation message and gave an invitation. More than a thousand people came rushing to the altar to receive Christ.

Toward the end of the meeting, a handsome, well-groomed gentleman stood in front of me. A missionary standing beside me started crying and shaking. He turned to me and said, "Brother Lowery, you see the gentleman standing in front of us? That is the mayor of our city. Would you pray for him that God would save his soul?" I walked down the platform and asked him, "Mr. Mayor, what are you seeking God for tonight?"

"Oh," he said, "I was here last night, and I saw what God did in this place. I want to serve the God who can do what I saw happen in this auditorium last night." I was able to lead him to Christ right then.

I tell you, people are tired of dead ritual, empty traditions, and stiff formality. They crave to see the power of a living Christ manifested in these last days. Hallelujah! As God manifests Himself through us, enabling us to have faith for great things, we will understand that *"with God all things are possible"* (Matthew 19:26).

Notes

1. Hank Hanegraff writes, "True Biblical faith...encapsulates three essential elements...*knowledge...agreement...trust*" (Hanegraff's emphasis). See his book *Christianity in Crisis* (Eugene, OR: Harvest House Publishers, 1993), 70.

2. Dennis Joseph Bennett and Rita Bennett, *The Holy Spirit and You: A Study Guide to the Spirit-Filled Life* (Plainfield, NJ: Logos International, 1971), 134.

3. Jack R. Taylor, *After the Spirit Comes* (Nashville, TN: Broadman Press, 1974), 91.

4. Eusebius Pamphilus, *Ecclesiastical History,* trans. Christian Frederick Cruse (Grand Rapids, MI: Baker Book House, 1977), 146.

Chapter 8

Gifts of Healing and Working of Miracles

HEALINGS, EXORCISMS, MIRACLES, and other signs and wonders confirmed Jesus as Messiah. After John the Baptist was arrested and imprisoned by Herod, he sent a message to his cousin, Jesus. John had started to question who Jesus was; everyone had expected the Messiah to be a conquering king but, surprisingly, He first came as a suffering servant. John wanted to know whether Jesus was the Messiah or if he and his followers should be looking for another. In reply, Jesus pointed to His accomplishments, saying,

> *Go back and report to John what you hear and see: the blind receive sight, the lame walk, those who have leprosy are cured, the deaf hear, the dead are raised, and the good news is preached to the poor.* *(Matthew 11:4–5)*

The message of the apostles also gained astonishing credibility through accompanying signs.

Paul described *"gifts of healing"* (1 Corinthians 12:9) and *"the working of miracles"* (v. 10 KJV) as two of the manifestations of the Spirit that serve an important purpose in the ongoing community of the risen Jesus, the church. Divine healing and the working of miracles provide an opportunity for the Christian message to be heard. If you want to share the Gospel, pray for the sick. When people are healed, they will ask about your God. Men and women will believe your message when they see the power of God confirming it.

GIFTS OF HEALING

Is the gift of healing like the gift of being an apostle, prophet, or evangelist? Are there some in the church who are healers? Does God give some the ability to heal? I do not believe this is what Paul teaches.

When Paul listed the manifestations of the Spirit, he literally referred to "gifts of healings."[1] This is the only component in Paul's list that he designated as *"gifts."* We should note that the words in the original for "gifts" and "healings" are both plural. Howard Ervin, theology professor at Oral Roberts University, explains, "Those who pray and lay hands on for healing...simply mediate the gift of healing from the Divine Healer to the sick person."[2] Therefore, it is the sick person who receives the benefit of the gift.

Jesus is the only Healer who exists in Christian circles.[3] As we faithfully turn to Him in prayer, He brings relief to those who are suffering. Jesus speaks of healing as a sign that will follow those who believe (Mark 16:17–18). As we share His Word with others, God endorses us with signs of His presence.

Every Spirit-filled Christian has the "potential for healing," illuminates the Reverend Francis MacNutt, but "for whatever reason, we all know that more people seem to get healed through the ministry of certain people than others."[4] God uses certain believers as channels of divine healing, just as He utilizes some people to teach the Word more clearly than others, and as He makes some believers more gifted in leading people to faith in Christ than others. This would explain why Paul included "gifts of healings" in both his list of manifestations of the Spirit in 1 Corinthians 12:9 and in his list of ministries mentioned later in the same chapter (v. 28).

Healing Manifests God's Compassion

It is no surprise to find gifts of healing among God's edifying gifts. The word *salvation* in Scripture alludes to much more than forgiveness of sin. The biblical idea includes deliverance from sin, God's wrath, and satanic bondage. It also implies healing of the complete person. Throughout the Scriptures, we see that God cares about the whole human being: body, mind, and spirit.

Physical ailments and hardship entered the world with sin (Genesis 3:16–19). In the Garden of Eden, there was no sickness. Man and woman were to be sustained by God, with continual access to the

Tree of Life. The rebellion of Adam and Eve ended all of that; as Paul correctly said, *"The wages of sin is death"* (Romans 6:23).

As God gathered a people, the nation of Israel, He revealed Himself as their Healer: *"I will not bring on you any of the diseases I brought on the Egyptians, for I am the LORD, who heals you"* (Exodus 15:26). God kept the Israelites well throughout their sojourn in the wilderness. Not only did their clothes not wear out, but their feet did not swell (Deuteronomy 8:4). To those who kept God's Law, God promised health and a long life: *"Worship the LORD your God, and his blessing will be on your food and water. I will take away sickness from among you....I will give you a full life span"* (Exodus 23:25–26).

God's assurance of healing for His people is found throughout the Bible. The psalmist glorified the Lord as the One who heals all our diseases:

> *Praise the LORD, O my soul; all my inmost being, praise his holy name. Praise the LORD, O my soul, and forget not all his benefits—who forgives all your sins and heals all your diseases, who redeems your life from the pit and crowns you with love and compassion.*
> *(Psalm 103:1–4)*

During the earthly ministry of Jesus, people knew the Nazarene as a healer. In the Gospel accounts, Christ expressed compassion through healing those who were sick. Jesus healed people by divine power before His suffering and death, and the evangelist Matthew applies Isaiah's prophecy in Isaiah 53:4, *"Surely He has borne our griefs and carried our sorrows,"* to Christ's ministry before the Cross:

> *When evening came, many who were demon-possessed were brought to him, and he drove out the spirits with a word and healed all the sick. This was to fulfill what was spoken through the prophet Isaiah: "He took up our infirmities and carried our diseases."*
> *(Matthew 8:16–17)*[5]

In addition to displaying Christ's mercy, these healings were something more. They were "proof," as Michael Green writes, "for those with eyes to see, for those whose prejudices do not blind them, that the Kingdom of God has broken in, that God's rule of wholeness has taken root."[6] As Jesus trained His disciples, He sent them to preach the Gospel. Each time, He also commanded them to heal the sick, cast out devils, and cleanse the lepers.[7]

Various types of healing are found in the Scriptures. First, there is spiritual healing: here we find the new birth and the healing of man's spiritual nature. Next, we have what some call "inner healing": the healing of our hearts, our minds, our emotions, and the mental scars of the past. Finally, the Bible describes physical healing. The Gospels and Acts record healings of blindness, deafness, skin disease, and other disorders. Some Christians depict deliverance from evil spirits as healing, while others categorize it as a working of miracles.[8]

Healing expresses God's boundless grace and unfailing love.[9] God is good, and He loves humanity. The Lord wants us to enjoy good health.[10] We know it is God's will for us to be made whole. If it were not God's will to heal us, turning to a doctor or medical science for help would also be wrong.[11] Thank heaven, this is not true. We can always confidently pray for God to heal us or someone else.

Why Healing May Be Delayed

However, healing may not always take place immediately. There are a number of reasons why this may be the case.[12] The moment may not be God's perfect timing. On occasion, God heals people instantaneously at the time of prayer. In other situations, sudden healing comes days, weeks, months, or years after prayer. Healing may happen as a process; it may occur gradually, over a period of time. We may need to pray for a person many times, and often for significant periods of time, to bring about healing.

For some situations, we may never see healing manifested in this life. Ultimately, at the Resurrection, all of us will receive our perfect healing. We will put on new, eternal, spiritual bodies. Jack Taylor writes, "I shall not be completely healed until I see Him and am made like Him. Until then, I live in a body which, barring my translation in the Rapture, will die." None of us completely sheds our sinful nature. We will not be made perfect until the coming of Jesus. Yet God continues to challenge us to surrender to Him and become more like Jesus. This is why Taylor concludes, "I am not, however, going to abandon the goal of wholeness and healing just because I am not yet physically perfect."[13]

We often overlook the fact that God has placed natural healing processes into the design of our bodies. While God does not always heal in a spectacular way, all healing is a manifestation of His graciousness. The moment we experience cuts, our bodies work toward healing. Our immune system fights the diseases that are all around us. God provides both natural healing and supernatural healing. Further, the assistance of medical science also comes from our heavenly Father; God imparts the knowledge used to create medicine.

God also wants us to take good care of ourselves. Our bodies are temples of the Holy Spirit. This means we are literally the house of God, His dwelling place. Most of us abuse God's house tremendously. We should eat moderately and according to a balanced diet. We should exercise and stay away from things that harm us. Taking care of God's temple means avoiding the excessive use of caffeine and the use of tobacco products and harmful drugs, including alcoholic beverages, that destroy our bodies. As good stewards of God's temples, we must use all the natural means at our disposal to care for our bodies and our health.[14]

The social environment in which we live also has an effect on our health.[15] Living in an unhappy home or with constant fighting in the workplace may bring on sickness. On the other hand, attending a healthy Spirit-led church will move us toward receiving the healing God desires for us.

Other reasons result in delayed healing. We need to pray specifically as the Spirit directs us; vague prayers bring vague answers. The Lord may postpone healing because we have allowed sins in our lives, although Jesus made it clear that sin is not always the reason for delayed healing (John 9:2–3). If we continue in sickness, we should ask God to search our hearts and cleanse us from anything that rebels against Him. Our sins may be subtle: unforgiveness, bitterness, jealousy, or hatred. The Holy Spirit will reveal them to us and bring us to repentance.

There are times when lack of faith may be the problem. The lack of faith could be either on the part of the one praying or the one being prayed for. Sometimes it could be both. Even medical science recognizes the importance of a so-called positive mental attitude. As we study the ministry of Jesus, we find occasions when the lack of faith of others seemed to limit what could be done through prayer. Nevertheless, lack of faith does not confine God. God has healed many unbelievers and brought them to faith in Christ.

Some Christians fail to seek healing from God because they have the mistaken belief that suffering with illness is sharing in the Cross with Christ. When the Bible speaks of sharing in Christ's suffering, it points to persecution, difficulty, and distress brought on by our obedience to the Gospel. Nowhere in the Bible does it say that sickness glorifies God. Michael Scanlon and Anne Shields define redemptive suffering as

> suffering imposed on us by others. It is martyrdom, torture, banishment, enslavement of Christians, and ridicule and deprivation of rights because of one's faith in Christ. Redemptive suffering is also the hardship borne for the sake of the Gospel: hunger, cold, shipwreck, and other such sufferings. It is trials and difficulties which strengthen and purify hearts. These forms of sufferings were borne by Jesus and his disciples.[16]

Looking at examples of healing in the New Testament, we realize that God does not use one particular method. Our experience proves this true. Sometimes, just as Jesus did, believers simply speak the words "Be healed." At other times, laying on of hands takes place; sometimes other actions prescribed by the Spirit are taken. The book of James gives instruction regarding anointing the sick with oil. The variety of ways that people are healed keeps us concentrating on the Great Physician, not our methods. God manifests His love for us through healing, inviting us, as George Martin suggests, "to greater faith and thanksgiving."[17]

A Testimony from the Dominican Republic

I would like to share a miraculous healing that God performed during my evangelistic crusade in the Dominican Republic. Great crowds attended the meetings each night. One evening, I had preached for about an hour and ministered to the needs of the people for an extended period. The meeting had exhausted me. Just as I was ready to close the service and leave the platform, my interpreter said, "Brother Lowery, can you pray for one more person?" I said to him, "I'm extremely tired and exhausted, but whom do you have?" At that very moment, some men were laying a man on the platform whose legs were drawn and twisted up under him. His arms were also twisted and drawn. He could neither walk nor use his arms. Every person in that great audience knew the man. People had moved him from one street corner to another, where he would beg for charity, which was his only means of support. As I walked over to lay hands on the man, suddenly the Lord pulled my hands back from him. God spoke to me and said, "I'm going to heal the man tonight, but don't lay your hands upon him. I must have all of the honor and all of the glory."

I am convinced that God would do more for us if we would be careful to give all of the praise and honor to Him. When I had experienced this unusual manifestation from God, I paused for a moment. I waited until all of the ministers and missionaries came around. Then I began to pray, *"Silver and gold have I none,"* words Peter and John spoke to the lame man in Acts 3:6 (KJV), a passage we have previously noted in our study. As I prayed that prayer, simultaneously, all of the other ministers and missionaries began to pray it with me: *"Silver and gold have I none; but such as I have give I thee: In the name of Jesus Christ of Nazareth rise up and walk"* (v. 6 KJV).

As we finished saying this, the man's legs and arms began to quake and jerk. The bones started to crack and pop. His legs straightened and so did his arms. We lifted him up on his feet. This hopeless paralytic, who had been bound and twisted all of his life, began to walk back and forth across the platform.

This healed man stretched his hands into the air. He praised God for his marvelous, miraculous deliverance. I have never seen an audience so affected as that great crowd was when they witnessed what God had done. Praise the Lord!

THE WORKING OF MIRACLES

Closely related to healings is the working of miracles. "The working of miracles covers those wonderful works which are not strictly healings," writes Regent University Bible scholar John Rea.[18] Some Christians place exorcisms in this category rather than in the category of healings. Raising the dead is in the category of miracles.

The root of the word used for "miracle" in 1 Corinthians 12:10 is the word *dunameon,* meaning "power." Any working of miracles is a display of God's power. This refers to any event, as James Dunn puts it, in which people and things are "visibly and beneficially affected in an extraordinary way by a non-rational power" through believers.[19] Just as Paul listed *"gifts of healing"* (1 Corinthians 12:9) rather than "a gift of healing," he also described *"the working of miracles"* (v. 10 KJV) rather than "the gift of being able to perform miracles." The gifts are the miracles themselves, not the permanent, ongoing power to perform miracles.[20]

Lee College professor Bill George writes, "A church that is faithful to the New Testament example will evidence faith in God's ability and willingness to do what men say is impossible."[21] Systematic theologian Colin Brown clarifies that "miracles function as a sign of identification, enabling the one who performs them to be identified as God's agent."[22] Many in our day dispute the possibility of miracles. They say that the laws of nature cannot be broken. However, as Michael Green points out, "a 'law of nature' is simply the name we give to a series of observed uniformities."[23]

Jesus cautions us to avoid undue attention to miracles. He rebuked people who were continually seeking a sign, saying, *"A wicked and adulterous generation asks for a miraculous sign!"* (Matthew 12:39). These same people failed to respond to the clear Word that God had already given. They just wanted to be amazed. Besides this, Christ warned against counterfeit miracles designed to lead people astray: *"False Christs and false prophets will appear and perform great signs and miracles to deceive even the elect—if that were possible. See, I have told you ahead of time"* (Matthew 24:24–25).

The New Testament records many miracles. Jesus turned the water into wine (John 2:1–11), walked on water (John 6:19), and called Lazarus from the grave (John 11:38–44). In the early church, the Spirit transported Philip from one place to the next (Acts 8:39–40), the dead were raised (Acts 9:40–41; Acts 20:9–12), and earthquakes took place at the right time to free Paul and Silas from prison (Acts 16:25–26).

The working of miracles in our midst always reminds us of God's greatness. God can do anything! As the prophet wrote, *"Ah, Sovereign LORD, you have made the heavens and the earth by your great power and outstretched arm. Nothing is too hard for you"* (Jeremiah 32:17).

MINISTERING DELIVERANCE FROM EVIL SPIRITS

The power of Jesus over evil spirits proves that "the Kingdom of God has invaded the realm of Satan to deal him a preliminary but decisive defeat," writes biblical theologian George Eldon Ladd.[24] While the ultimate establishment of God's kingdom will come at the end of the age, Christ established a beachhead at His first coming. Michael Green phrases it another way: "The expulsion of dark forces was then, and is now, a spectacular aspect of the coming of the Kingdom of God."[25]

The Bible paints our world as one of constant spiritual battle. Evil spirits continually wage war against those who follow God. For this reason, Paul instructed Christians to wear their spiritual armor

(Ephesians 6:10–18). This means that we are to speak the truth and remain in a right relationship with God. To stay protected, we should unceasingly share the Gospel. Practicing our faith shields us from demonic attack. Immersing ourselves in God's Word helps us to defeat the Enemy.

Jesus said that believers would *"drive out demons"* (Mark 16:17). People often ask me how a Christian should respond when confronted with someone they believe is demon-possessed. First, we must always exercise great caution. God is infinitely more powerful than Satan; but the Devil has been around a long time, and demonic forces are powerful.

Secondly, we need a manifestation of discernment to make an accurate spiritual diagnosis.[26] Again, observe how the manifestations of the Spirit work together. Not every sickness is caused by demon possession. Neither is every situation that seems demonic really so.

I would insist that individuals who want to venture into ministering this kind of deliverance should be absolutely sure of their relationships with God. Make sure you deal quickly with any unconfessed sin. Just admit your faults to God, and the Lord will cleanse you. If you do not, you will find it impossible to fight the Devil. However, when you are in full fellowship with God, you can declare, "In the name of Jesus Christ, come out, you demonic spirit." Stand firm on the Word of God. The ministers of deliverance must recognize their authority in Christ and take authority in the name of Jesus.

You should also be grounded in the teaching of the Scriptures and approach the situation very prayerfully. You must be fully confident of God's protection, guaranteed in His Word. Whoever exorcises an evil spirit must be empowered by the Holy Spirit.

As in any spiritual battle, we must do as James instructed: if we submit ourselves to God and resist the Devil, he must flee (James 4:7).

Deal differently with each person influenced or possessed by demonic forces. There is no certain formula or pattern that a person can follow and expect results. We are all in a spiritual battle, and the time to prepare is now.

SIGNS AND WONDERS, AND THE CONFIRMATION OF THE GOSPEL

During my ministry, God has graciously confirmed the preaching of the Gospel with signs and wonders. This should be no surprise. The book of Acts is full of such accounts. There is nothing special about me or anyone else God uses, except for the fact that we place ourselves in His hands as available vessels.

For a number of years I have preached at camp meetings and conventions throughout the world. One particular summer, I was scheduled to preach at several camp meetings. While ministering at one in Kentucky, something wondrous happened. Suddenly, a heavy cloud came inside the tabernacle. The cloud would stand still for a moment over a group of people. Then the Holy Spirit would move mightily upon everybody underneath that cloud. The people were visibly shaken: some were weeping, others were falling out under the power.

The cloud would move to different places in the tabernacle. As the cloud shifted, it would affect the people wherever it settled. God healed people. Some folks jumped out of their wheelchairs, delivered. The demonstration of God's power was visible. You could see the cloud and witness the repercussions. That awesome exhibition of the Holy Spirit touched many people. There was such a sense of God's presence that gripped that congregation. Sinners screamed under conviction. People sitting in their cars outside jumped out of their cars and ran in under the tabernacle; those standing around outside the tabernacle ran in also. They were shouting, weeping, falling on their faces, and crying out to God for deliverance and salvation. It was truly a phenomenal outpouring and manifestation of the Spirit. A similar marvel happened again at the camp meeting in Maryland that summer.

A Testimony from India

Manifestations of healings and miracles have accentuated my ministry all around the world. As you follow Christ and are nourished by His Word, you too will see His power work through you. Some years ago, I was in India for an evangelistic crusade. One evening as I was ministering, the Holy Spirit moved across the great audience. There was a manifestation of God's glory; again, a visible cloud appeared over the audience.

A leper, who was standing at the edge of the great crowd, began running around the audience. Finally, he jumped onto the platform and took the microphone from my hand and began to shout at the top of his voice, in his language, "I'm healed! I'm healed! I'm healed!" I asked my interpreter to tell me what he was saying. The man, a resident of a leper colony, had been in the last stage of leprosy. The leper colony was about a hundred miles from where we were, but he had heard about the crusade and had asked permission to come, saying, "I believe that if I can get to that meeting, I will be healed of my leprosy." The officials had refused to grant permission because of his serious condition. Nevertheless, he had slipped away from the leper colony and had walked and hitchhiked rides until finally he arrived at the meeting.

Standing at the back of the crowd, where more than forty thousand people had gathered to worship God, this leper had suddenly looked down at his hands and had seen the leprosy departing from his body. It was just like turning on the defroster in your car and watching it defrost the windshield. That is the way he would afterward describe his miracle. He said, "I saw the leprosy departing." While he was giving his testimony, rejoicing, leaping, and dancing, the audience was greatly moved. Hundreds rushed forward to receive Christ as their personal Savior.

At the close of the service, a gentleman came up to me and said, "You're to come to my home tomorrow morning and pray for my son. He is seven years of age and is an invalid. He has never walked a step in his life. I own the newspaper company in this city. If your God will heal my son, I will become a Christian and turn all of my assets over to the Christian religion. I will do everything I can to help to propagate Christianity throughout the whole of India."

I responded, "Sir, I will be happy to come and minister to your son. But if he is healed, it will be through the power of our Lord Jesus Christ, God's only Son, the only Savior of mankind."

Very early the next morning, the man's driver came to where I was staying and drove me to his house. I thought I would be there only for a few minutes and then return to my room for rest. When I arrived, I saw to my amazement that the yard was full of people. People filled the porch and house. I pushed my way through the crowd and into the house to minister to the young boy.

Before I prayed, I felt I must talk about Jesus. As we have studied, the Bible says that faith comes by hearing, and hearing by the Word of God (Romans 10:17). While I was sharing God's Word, I discerned that faith was beginning to rise in the room. I looked across the room. The Lord revealed to me that a lady who was sitting in the back of the room was suffering from excruciating pain and an extremely high fever. Led by the Spirit, I described the lady's condition to the group. She screamed out,

"That's true, but how did you know?" I answered, "The Lord Jesus Christ, the Son of God, revealed it to me by His Spirit." Then I proclaimed, "And now you are healed in the name of Jesus! Your pain is gone! Your fever is gone!" She began to scream and rejoice, saying, "I am healed! I am healed! The fever is gone! The pain is gone!"

After that healing took place, faith soared even higher. I said to the father of the boy, "It is now time to pray for your son." He brought the boy to me and placed him in my arms. This young man was one of the most handsome lads that I have ever seen in my life. His legs were like rubber, and he had absolutely no control over them. After I had prayed for him, I felt a witness and a confirmation of the Holy Spirit that God had healed his body.

I handed him back to his father and said, "I believe your son is healed. You will have to teach him to walk like you would train an infant, because he has never walked in his life." The father said, "No, if your God has healed my son, he can walk."

At that moment, God once again reminded me about the man at the gate called Beautiful in the third chapter of Acts. After the Holy Spirit led Peter and John to say, *"In the name of Jesus Christ of Nazareth rise up and walk"* (v. 6 KJV), the man jumped up and walked. His ankle bones received strength, and he went into the temple, leaping and praising God. This man had been lame from birth. Nobody had to send him to walking school or train him to walk. I said, "Lord, if You did it for a man who was over forty years old, you can certainly do it for this seven-year-old lad."

I walked across the room with the lad in my arms. As I put him down on the floor, I said, "Son, when I release you, I want you to walk across this room to where your father is." The boy not only walked, he ran and leaped into his father's arms.

Healing is real! Miracles are real! The gifts of the Spirit are real. Enjoy and experience the manifestations of the Holy Spirit in your life.

Notes

1. Howard Matthew Ervin, *Spirit Baptism: A Biblical Investigation* (Peabody, MA: Hendrickson Publishers, 1987), 106–109.

2. Ibid., 91.

3. See James Douglas Grant Dunn, *Jesus and the Spirit: A Study of the Religious and Charismatic Experience of Jesus and the First Christians as Reflected in the New Testament* (Philadelphia: The Westminster Press, 1975), 24.

4. Francis MacNutt, *The Power to Heal* (Notre Dame, IN: Ave Maria Press, 1977), 91.

5. John Rea, *The Holy Spirit in the Bible: All the Major Passages about the Spirit—A Commentary* (Altamonte Springs, FL: Creation House, 1990), 125.

6. Edward Michael Bankers Green, *Who Is This Jesus?* (Nashville, TN: Thomas Nelson Publishers, 1992), 41.

7. Tommy Lee Osborn, *Healing the Sick* (Tulsa, OK: Osborne Foundation, 1959), 49.

8. Francis MacNutt, *Healing*, 2d ed. (New York: Doubleday, 1990), 165.

9. The Hebrew word *chesed* means God's unfailing covenant love. No matter what happened, God had chosen to love His people. In the writings of the New Testament, *charis*, grace, also represents the infinite love God has for humankind.

10. George Martin, *Healing: Reflections on the Gospel* (Ann Arbor, MI: Servant Books, 1977), 30.

11. Jack R. Taylor, *The Word of God with Power* (Nash-ville, TN: Broadman and Holdman, Publishers, 1993), 74.

12. See Francis MacNutt's section on the eleven reasons why he believes people are not healed in *Healing*, 2d ed. (New York: Doubleday, 1990), 251–263. In explaining "now is not the time," he outlines how the period of healing varies.

13. Taylor, *The Word of God with Power*, 73.

14. See George Martin, *Healing*, 35–36, and Francis MacNutt, *Healing*, 258, 160.

15. MacNutt, *Healing*, 262.

16. Michael Scanlon and Anne Therese Shields, *And Their Eyes Were Opened: Encountering Jesus in the Sacraments* (Notre Dame, IN: The Word of Life, 1976), 96.

17. Martin, *Healing*, 37–38.

18. Rea, *The Holy Spirit in the Bible*, 251.

19. Dunn, *Jesus and the Spirit*, 210.

20. Ibid., 211.

21. Bill George, *Added to the Church: A Church of God Membership Manual* (Cleveland, TN: Pathway Press, 1987), 18.

22. Colin Brown, *Miracles and the Critical Mind* (Grand Rapids, MI: William B. Eerdmans Publishing Company, 1984), 19.

23. Green, *Who is This Jesus?*, 46.

24. George Eldon Ladd, *The Presence of the Future* (Grand Rapids, MI: William B. Eerdmans Publishing Company, 1974), 151.

25. Edward Michael Bankers Green, *I Believe in the Holy Spirit* (Grand Rapids, MI: William B. Eerdmans Publishing Company, 1975), 42.

26. For a discussion about interviewing the people being prayed for, consult Francis MacNutt's fine books on healing: *Healing* and *The Power to Heal*. See also John Wimber and Kevin Springer, *Power Healing* (New York: Harper and Row, 1987) and Charles H. Kraft, *Christianity with Power: Your Worldview and Your Experience of the Supernatural* (Ann Arbor, MI: Vine Books, 1989).

Chapter 9

PROPHECY AND THE HOLY SPIRIT

W HEN MOST PEOPLE hear the word *prophecy*, they think of foretelling the future. In Christian circles, believers frequently re-gard prophecies as predictions concerning the coming of Christ and the final Judgment. While that is part of what constitutes prophecy, in the Bible, prophecy often involved "forthtelling" rather than foretelling. A prophet was one who heard from God and delivered God's message to others. *"Everyone who prophesies speaks to men for their strengthening, encouragement and comfort"* (1 Corinthians 14:3).

The 100th archbishop of Canterbury, Michael Ramsey, sees a continued prophetic role for the church of Jesus Christ:

> Prophecy is the power to discern the will and purpose of God and to declare it; a Church that lives after the Spirit will have this gift diffused among its members; it will be a prophetic Church; it will be a Church sometimes able to say with conviction, *"It seemed good to the Holy Spirit and to us"* (Acts 15:28).[1]

119

The Hebrew word for prophet was *nabi*. Scholars believe it was closely related to *nabu*, a word in the ancient Assyrian and Babylonian language Akkadian, meaning "to call." It came to depict one who preached and proclaimed what God wanted to be said; the Lord was the source of the message. The Israelites also used other terms for prophets, including *"seer"* (1 Samuel 9:9) and *"man of God"* (2:27).

The Greeks used the word *prophetes,* meaning "one who speaks beforehand," in an exclusively religious sense. Our word *prophet* is simply a transliteration of the Greek. *Prophetes* came from two words. The prefix *pro* means "before." *Phetes* means "speaker" and is derived from the verb *phanai*, which means "to speak, say, or proclaim." Words derived from the root word *phe* were always used in a religious connotation. In Greek society, these prophets, or oracles, were the mouthpieces of the gods.[2] The Christian use of the term referred to those who brought an inspired word from the Lord.

When Paul used the word *prophecy*, he understood it as a "word of revelation."[3] The gift of prophecy differs from "a God-given ability to preach and teach the gospel effectively."[4] Paul's idea of prophecy was a "spontaneous utterance, a revelation given in words to the prophet to be delivered as it is given."[5]

Some Christian commentators argue that the New Testament idea of prophecy is exclusively preaching and sharing the Christian message. Yet other Greek words (*kerygma, evangelion, angelia*) are used in the New Testament for proclamation or preaching.[6] The context of Paul's discussion could hardly support such a limited perspective.

At times, prophecy may take place through inspired preaching. In my own ministry, God has redirected my message many times. I knew what I was saying was not from me but from God. Prophetic preaching happens as we allow the Holy Spirit to lead us in the preparation and delivery of a message. Also, God will speak to people directly through our words as we share our faith with others or counsel with them. Nevertheless, Paul was primarily referring to a special, clear, spontaneous message from God to His gathered people.

OLD COVENANT PROPHETS

Throughout the Bible, men and women walked and talked with God. God sought them out. From Enoch to Noah, Abraham to Joseph, and Elijah to Malachi, godly people received God's message and shared it with others. At a time when the Israelites were in slavery, God chose a prophet among them: Moses. Moses brought them deliverance, and God used him to deliver His holy Law. Looking forward to the coming of the Messiah, Moses asserted that there would be another prophet like himself who would come. Moses stated his desire for all of God's people to be prophets: *"I wish that all the Lord's people were prophets and that the LORD would put his Spirit on them!"* (Numbers 11:29).

At first, God ruled His people through judges. Then the Israelites became envious of other nations and asked God for a king so they could be like all their neighbors. Although God wanted to be their King, He granted them this request and used the prophet Samuel to choose the first two kings of Israel: Saul and, later, David.

God raised up the prophets Elijah and Elisha to remind people of His great power. He commissioned other prophets, such as Isaiah, Jeremiah, and Ezekiel, to warn the people of God against disobedience and resulting judgment, as well as to encourage them with the hope of ultimate restoration, the coming of a Messiah, and a new covenant.

NEW COVENANT PROPHETS

Jesus fulfilled the Old Testament prophecies of a coming Messiah, functioning as Prophet, Priest, and King. After His death and resurrection, He appointed His church to carry on His work, including the work of prophecy.

Under the old covenant, the Spirit would come upon the prophet, apparently for a season, and then leave after the prophet had relayed God's word or fulfilled a particular task. John the Baptist was the final prophet under the old covenant. In the new covenant, the Spirit of God comes and continues to abide, and the anointing remains.

Any believer could be used to prophesy in the New Testament church, as Paul instructed: *"For you can all prophesy in turn"* (1 Corinthians 14:31). This means that any believer who is surrendered to Christ and His Spirit may be an instrument to manifest a prophetic word from God. Paul, Luke, and others show us through the instruction and recorded events in their writings that there was a recognized ministry of being a prophet, just as one might be a pastor, teacher, evangelist, or apostle. This person would be one through whom God would frequently speak. This prophet's lifestyle would validate the messages, and these prophetic messages would always be consistent with the teachings of Scripture.

GENERAL REVELATION

God reveals Himself in two ways. First, God can be found in general revelation, in the world around us. He is found in creation. We recognize His creativity through His design of the vast universe in which we live. We may discover God in the smallest object known to humanity, the sub-particles of the atom. The apostle Paul wrote:

> *For since the creation of the world God's invisible qualities—his eternal power and divine nature—have been clearly seen, being understood from what has been made, so that men are without excuse.* (Romans 1:20)

SPECIAL REVELATION

Secondly, God specifically speaks through what we call special revelation: through His Word, through direct communication with humankind. In the opening chapter of Genesis, we read that God created the universe through His word. The Old Testament prophets brought the word of the Lord to the people. The first chapter of John's gospel describes the Lord Jesus as *"the Word"* (v. 1) who was with God in the beginning and who is, in fact, God. This Word became a human being and lived among us. Later, the followers of the crucified and risen Christ shared the Old Testament Scriptures and the life and words of Jesus concerning the way to salvation. When we share our faith using the Scriptures, we are sharing God's dynamic Word. Moreover, as I indicated earlier, God can also speak to people directly through our words—whether we are sharing our faith one to one, or one to multitudes of people.

We call the Bible the Word of God. This inspired collection of ancient documents reliably and faithfully records God's acts and deeds in history. We call Scripture the Canon—the measuring rod or standard by which we judge all things concerning Christian faith and practice.

Paul said, *"Two or three prophets should speak, and the others should weigh carefully what is said"* (1 Corinthians 14:29). The other believers' understanding of Scripture plays a crucial role in evaluating the prophet's word. John told us to judge the prophet by the prophecy and teaching he brings: *"Every spirit that acknowledges that Jesus Christ has come in the flesh is from God, but every spirit that does not acknowledge Jesus is not from God. This is the spirit of the antichrist"* (1 John 4:2–3). As

Jack Taylor writes, "God has spoken; to acknowledge that is basic. God is still speaking; to deny that is tragic. God is consistent, which means that He never violates former revelation with subsequent revelation."[7] Or as David Watson clarifies,

> The Spirit is not confined to the Word; He speaks to us in a great variety of ways apart from the Scriptures; but these will not be at variance with the Scriptures, which are for us the supreme objective authority of God's self-revelation.[8]

Paul instructed believers to *"be eager to prophesy"* (1 Corinthians 14:39). While Christian congregations always need to be open to the manifestation of prophecy, false and misdirected prophecies occur constantly. Some individuals will use the guise of prophecy to gain control over others. Inexperienced believers need to learn to distinguish between their thoughts and the voice of God. Well-meaning but mistaken prophets must be gently corrected and encouraged. We must expose false prophets in light of Scripture.

One thing the apostle made clear: within the context of gathered believers, *"everything should be done in a fitting and orderly way"* (1 Corinthians 14:40). Unlike the ecstatic prophets of the early Montanist movement and the pagan oracles of false religions, *"the spirits of prophets are subject to the control of prophets"* (v. 32).

LEARNING TO LISTEN TO GOD

God may speak through any Christian. Experience and reliance on God, combined with the discernment of spirits, enable us to hear God's voice. We must start by learning how to hear God in our own prayer closets. While the Bible reveals that God has at times spoken through animals and unbelievers, they were the exceptions.

Jesus said, *"Remain in me, and I will remain in you. No branch can bear fruit by itself; it must remain in the vine. Neither can you bear fruit unless you remain in me"* (John 15:4). If we want to hear God speak to us, we must develop our relationships with Him by spending time with Him. Then, truly, as His sheep, we will know His voice and follow Him (10:2–5). As we dwell in His teaching, we *"will know the truth, and the truth will set* [us] *free"* (8:32).

Notes

1. Michael Ramsey, *Holy Spirit* (Grand Rapids, MI: William B. Eerdmans Publishing Company, 1977), 84.

2. Colin Brown, "Prophet," in *The New International Dictionary of New Testament Theology (NIDNTT)*, ed. Colin Brown (Grand Rapids, MI: Zondervan Publishing House, 1978), 3:74–77.

3. James Douglas Grant Dunn, *Jesus and the Spirit: A Study of the Religious and Charismatic Experience of Jesus and the First Christians as Reflected in the New Testament* (Philadelphia: The Westminster Press, 1975), 228.

4. John Rea, *The Holy Spirit in the Bible: All the Major Passages about the Spirit—A Commentary* (Altamonte Springs, FL: Creation House, 1990), 252.

5. Dunn, *Jesus and the Spirit*, 228. See also Jack R. Taylor, *The Word of God with Power* (Nashville, TN: Broadman and Holdman, Publishers, 1993), 117.

6. Colin Brown, "Proclamation, Preach, Kerygma," in *NIDNTT*, 3:44–68.

7. Taylor, *The Word of God with Power*, 40.

8. David Watson, *I Believe in the Church* (Grand Rapids, MI: William B. Eerdmans Publishing Company, 1978), 171–172.

Chapter 10

SPEAKING WITH TONGUES

I MAGINE HOW YOU would have felt if you were in that upstairs room in Jerusalem where Jesus' followers were staying after His ascension to heaven. The apostles probably reminded one another, "Jesus told us that we would receive power from on high." (See Acts 1:8.) They prayed, yet as time passed, nothing supernatural was happening among them. They probably encouraged one another, saying things like, "The Master told us to wait in Jerusalem for the gift He said the Father would send. This gift will come." (See verses 4–5.)

Finally, the Day of Pentecost came, and

suddenly a sound like the blowing of a violent wind came from heaven and filled the whole house where they were sitting. They saw what seemed to be tongues of fire that separated and came to rest on each of them. All of them were filled with the Holy Spirit and began to speak in other tongues as the Spirit enabled them.
(Acts 2:2–4)

The church of Jesus Christ has never been the same since.

This assembly, now empowered by the Holy Spirit, quickly expanded and turned the world upside down. As others turned to Christ, they too received this power of the Holy Spirit. Throughout the book of Acts, Luke usually referred to an occurrence of tongues as accompanying this immersion in the Holy Spirit.

Consequently, most Pentecostal and many charismatic groups define speaking in tongues as the "initial evidence" or the "initial physical evidence" of the baptism in the Holy Spirit. Throughout the twentieth century, a debate has raged about whether or not tongues is the initial sign of the release of the Holy Spirit. Some speak of this manifestation as a "frequent consequence of baptism in the Spirit."

The word we translate "to speak in tongues" is *glossolalia*, from the Greek words *glossais*, "tongues," and *lalein*, "to speak." Literally, the word is "tongues speaking." In both Greek and English, the word *tongues* simply connotes "languages."

On the Day of Pentecost, Jewish people from throughout the Roman Empire had gathered in Jerusalem for the feast. When the ascended Jesus clothed His followers with heavenly power, observers of these disciples heard them praise God in languages from various parts of the world. Some say that this was a case of *akoulalia,* the perceived hearing of another language even when one is not spoken.[1] The most straightforward and common interpretation is that these followers of the risen Jesus engaged in *xenolalia,* which is the speaking of a language known in some part of the world, but not known by the speaker.[2] However, this was not, as some have suggested, a supernatural preaching of the Gospel in other languages never learned; the manifestation of tongues here was an act of corporate praise and worship. Afterward, Peter, in his own language, proclaimed the Gospel to all who were there.[3]

Yet there are accounts of people throughout church history who have preached the Gospel in a language they did not learn. This would be classified more as a miracle than as a manifestation of tongues.[4] There are also cases in which people have spoken in tongues in languages known by other people, and this has often been a catalyst to bring them to faith. I have had this experience many times in my ministry in various parts of the world. This may be an example of tongues as a sign for the unbeliever (1 Corinthians 14:22).[5]

Was the manifestation of speaking in tongues at Pentecost a once-in-a-lifetime sign or something more? Jesus said that speaking in new tongues would be one sign that would identify believers in Him (Mark 16:17). Speaking in tongues is also mentioned in Paul's list of manifestations of the Spirit in 1 Corinthians 12. In 1 Corinthians 14, the apostle described the proper use of tongues in the corporate gathering of the church as well as a devotional, private use of this manifestation.

TONGUES OF MEN AND OF ANGELS

Was the speaking in tongues that Paul depicted the same manifestation as the one that occurred at Pentecost, or was it a different kind? Luke records the account of the Day of Pentecost in the book of Acts. He was also Paul's companion for a time. Most likely, the tongues described by Luke were the same manifestation experienced by Paul (1 Corinthians 14:18) and the churches to which Paul ministered. This seems particularly likely since Luke used the same term as Paul. The only possible difference may be that Paul expanded the definition of tongues to include angelic languages besides human ones (13:1).

Paul explained that utterance in tongues is the speaking of *"mysteries"* (14:2) unto God. Paul wrote about prayer in tongues and called it praying in the Spirit. He wrote about singing and blessing in tongues and described it as singing and blessing in the Spirit (vv. 14–15). From Paul's exposition, we understand that speaking in tongues is primarily a form of prayer.

As British professor C. F. D. Moule writes, the manifestation of tongues is a "significant outlet of pent-up praise or emotion too deep, too intense, for words: it is a precious mode of private devotion. It relaxes and releases the soul for adoration."[6] Lutheran pastor Larry Christenson speaks of receiving a language with which he could praise God continually.[7] Presbyterian charismatic theologian and professor J. Rodman Williams speaks of tongues as "declaring the works of God in ways transcending all human ability."[8] Baptist theologian Howard Ervin writes that Leon Cardinal Suenens, Catholic Primate of Belgium, describes tongues as a form of "non-discursive prayer" that he compares with the "gift of tears" and "abstract art." Ervin sees this manifestation as a "supernatural means of taming the restless evil of the tongue."[9] Anglican minister Michael Green regards the purpose of tongues as enabling "the recipient to pray to God from the depths of his being and not merely from the conscious levels of his mind."[10] Paul may have been speaking about prayer in tongues when he wrote in Romans 8:26–27:

> *In the same way, the Spirit helps us in our weakness. We do not know what we ought to pray for, but the Spirit himself intercedes for us with groans that words cannot express. And he who searches our hearts knows the mind of the Spirit, because the Spirit intercedes for the saints in accordance with God's will.*

German New Testament scholar Ernst Käsemann believes that this phenomenon of *"groans that words cannot express"* is speaking in tongues. Käsemann points out from this Scripture passage that praying in tongues does not reveal the power and wealth of the Christian community but its weakness. Käsemann expands on his insights. He writes, "In this," that is, praying in tongues,

> the Spirit manifests himself as the intercessor of the community before God and he takes it up into his intercession....Prayer is made for the

whole of enslaved and oppressed creation. The intercession of the exalted Christ takes place at the right hand of God. The Spirit...is the earthly presence of the exalted Lord and does his work, intercession included, in the sphere and through the ministry of the community.[11]

Over the years, I have come to value speaking with other tongues as praying in the Spirit. When we don't know how to pray as we should, then the Holy Spirit becomes an intercessor for us. The Spirit of God prays to the Father on our behalf. He presents our deepest needs to the heavenly Father in a way in which we are unable. Speaking in tongues is a verbalized manifestation of prayer in the Spirit. Many who speak in tongues sense a release in prayer to express to God what they are unable to say using their usual vocabularies. Studies have proven that those who speak in tongues are not any more psychologically unstable than any other group of people. It may be possible that those who speak in tongues enjoy generally better mental health.[12]

Paul said to *"pray in the Spirit on all occasions"* (Ephesians 6:18). He probably meant that we are not only to pray in our native language as we are guided by the Spirit but also in tongues. Jude made reference to praying *"in the Holy Spirit"* (Jude 20), which may also be, at least in part, a reference to praying in tongues.

When we speak in tongues, are we speaking a language? I believe that Scripture teaches we are. It may be a human language or an angelic one. Sometimes it may be like baby talk between you and God.

Speaking with Tongues

At other times, it may be a brilliantly constructed petition in a human language you have never learned. Tongues gives a voice to our spirits. As Harold Horton explains, "It has nothing whatever to do with linguistic ability, nor with the mind or intellect of man. It is a manifestation of the mind of the Spirit of God employing human speech organs."[13]

Using the Gift of Tongues

Paul asked the question, *"Do all speak in tongues?"* (1 Corinthians 12:30). From the context, the answer is no. We ponder, "Then are tongues available to all?" One answer we often hear is this: Not all speak in tongues at a public level. Some teach that certain people receive the gift of tongues, by which they mean a ministry of speaking in tongues in the assembly of believers. Paul did list those who speak in tongues along with other ministry gifts, such as apostle, prophet, or teacher.

It may be that God has called some to bring an utterance in tongues more frequently than others in the congregation. It could also be that Paul was saying that the ministry performed by an apostle is different from that of a brother or sister who brings forth an utterance in tongues.

Perhaps you have heard people say that tongues are the least of the gifts. You won't find that in the Bible. Holy Writ does say that prophecy is superior to tongues in the congregational setting, unless someone interprets (1 Corinthians 14:5). However, the Bible never denigrates the manifestation of tongues as useless. Through tongues, the Lord gives believers the ability to build themselves up in the Spirit.

Speaking in tongues is a marvelous gift to us from God, but some appear to consider *glossolalia* more important than coming to know Jesus and other things God has commanded. To hear them talk, receiving tongues is the full Gospel. We must worship the Giver of all gifts, never the gifts themselves.

Then there is also the other extreme. Some consider tongues to be foolishness, mere psychological trickery or even a counterfeit from Satan.[14] They frequently speak harshly of the "tongues movement." Others label Pentecostalism a cult. These utterances of tongues, produced by the Spirit, may seem foolish to some. Yet to those who experience these manifestations, they are anything but foolish. Testimony after testimony points to the exercise of tongues as resulting in a closer walk with the Lord and a more meaningful relationship with Him. In addition, to answer the charge that tongues is a counterfeit of Satan, we must ask, "If we ask God for a good gift, will He give us a snake instead?" He would not! (See Matthew 7:9–11.)

Some critics of speaking in tongues have convinced themselves that tongues disappeared from the church after the apostolic age, never to return. They base their understanding on a faulty interpretation of Paul's statement in 1 Corinthians 13:10: *"When perfection comes, the imperfect disappears."*

As I noted earlier, the apostle was describing the Second Coming, not the canonization of Scripture or the establishment of the church. In this same passage, Paul, in comparing the eternal and enduring nature of love to temporal things, spoke of how prophecies, knowledge, and tongues will eventually pass from the scene. Knowledge certainly has not passed from the scene, and Paul never said that prophecy and tongues would cease operating in the church before the return of Christ.

Some commentators say that the tongues that are spoken today and the tongues that were spoken at Corinth differ from the manifestation of tongues that occurred at Pentecost, which is recorded in the book of Acts. They argue that Corinthian and modern tongues were "worked up" by frenzied believers.[15] Paul made no distinction between tongues in this way; the apostle merely guided the Corinthian church to keep the practice in perspective.

More kindly critics of an exaggerated emphasis on tongues warn believers neither to forbid nor to seek them.[16] This position is charitable toward those who speak in tongues and recognizes the perpetuity of spiritual gifts, although, regrettably, it also leads believers not to seek something God has made available for their benefit.

Paul urged the Corinthians, *"I would like every one of you to speak in tongues"* (1 Corinthians 14:5), not so they could impress him with their spirituality but so they could be edified and then be able to bring a prophetic message to the church. It is true that we are to desire the greater gifts (1 Corinthians 12:31), such as prophecy (14:1), for use in the church. Yet do not be afraid to manifest what God gives, either in your private devotion or in public gatherings.

The Purpose of Tongues

What is the purpose of speaking in tongues? Commentator John Rea lists five purposes: It is a sign of the outpouring of the Holy Spirit. It is "a means of personal edification through the communication of our spirits with God in praise and prayer." It enhances congregational worship as people enter into spiritual praise and worship. It is a sign to strangers and unbelievers that God is among His people. Finally, in gatherings of believers, tongues and their interpretation strengthen the church.[17]

Sometime after I was baptized in the Spirit, God used me to deliver a public manifestation of tongues to a congregation. He also enabled me to engage in the interpretation of tongues. Both gifts have been very prominent during most of the years of my ministry.

Reading through Paul's instructions to the tongues-speaking church in Corinth, you may be disturbed by what he said in 1 Corinthians 14:22: *"Tongues, then, are a sign, not for believers but for unbelievers; prophecy, however, is for believers, not for unbelievers."* This seems contradictory to what he wrote in the next verse:

Speaking with Tongues

So if the whole church comes together and everyone speaks in tongues, and some who do not understand or some unbelievers come in, will they not say that you are out of your mind?   *(v. 23)*

As Howard Ervin writes,

Even to the casual reader there is an apparent inconsistency in this verse....This apparent ambiguity makes it one of the most difficult to interpret of all the passages relating to the charismatic manifestations of the Holy Spirit.[18]

However, as we study this section of Scripture carefully, and in context, we get an overall understanding of the proper use of tongues in the assembly of believers. We discover that the goal in these times of public gatherings is for outsiders to say, *"God is really among you!"* (1 Corinthians 14:25), rather than thinking that Christians are insane (vv. 23–25). For this reason, prophecy has priority over a public utterance of tongues, unless it is followed by interpretation.

INTERPRETATION OF TONGUES

The apostle Paul insisted that when speaking in tongues takes place in the assembly, someone should interpret the utterance. This exercise is not necessarily "an exact translation" but an "interpretation."[19] Assembly of God professor Russell Spittler explains that interpretation "is the spiritual gift (*charisma*) by which one so endowed makes clear to the congregation the unintelligible utterance of one who has spoken in tongues" and is "no less extraordinary than other charisma."[20]

Quite often, the interpretation seems to take longer than the utterance itself. Having traveled the world over, I do not find that strange. Frequently, a short expression in one language takes much longer to explain in another. Anglican Dennis Bennett has an additional answer, that the interpretation of the original utterance was followed by additional words of prophecy.[21] The prophetic word may be an answer to the previous prayer in tongues.[22]

For speaking in tongues to be a part of public worship, someone should always interpret the utterance in tongues. Otherwise, the manifestation fails to build up and encourage the gathered believers. Paul wrote:

> *If anyone speaks in a tongue, two—or at the most three—should speak, one at a time, and someone must interpret. If there is no interpreter, the speaker should keep quiet in the church and speak to himself and God.*
> *(1 Corinthians 14:27–28)*

In the public setting, if anyone speaks in tongues, the congregation should pray for an interpretation. We should never be so rigid that the Spirit is prohibited from operating. We must never forget the apostle's warning: *"Be eager to prophesy, and do not forbid speaking in tongues"* (v. 39).

Notes

1. See John Rodman Williams, *The Gift of the Holy Spirit Today: The Greatest Reality of the Twentieth Century* (Plainfield, NJ: Logos International, 1980), 31. Russell Spittler defines the term *akoulalia* (also called *akolalia*) in his article "Glossolalia," in *Dictionary of Pentecostal and Charismatic Movements,* ed. Stanley M. Burgess, Gary B. McGee, and Patrick H. Alexander (Grand Rapids, MI: Zondervan Publishing House, 1988), 336.

2. Spittler, "Glossolalia," 336.

3. Arthur Wallis, *Pray in the Spirit: The Work of the Holy Spirit in the Ministry of Prayer* (Fort Washington, PA: Christian Literature Crusade, 1970), 84.

4. Charles Peter Wagner, *Your Spiritual Gifts Can Help Your Church Grow: How to Find Your Gift and Use It* (Glendale, CA: Gospel Light Regal Books, 1979), 236.

5. Harald Bredesen and Pat King, *Yes, Lord* (Plainfield, NJ: Logos International, 1972), 199.

6. Charles Francis Digby Moule, *The Holy Spirit* (Grand Rapids, MI: William B. Eerdmans Publishing Company, 1978), 87.

7. Larry Christenson, *Speaking in Tongues and Its Significance for the Church* (Minneapolis, MN: Dimension Books, 1968), 13.

8. John Rodman Williams, *The Pentecostal Reality* (Plainfield, NJ: Logos International, 1972), 3.

9. Howard Matthew Ervin, *And Forbid Not to Speak with Tongues* (Plainfield, NJ: Logos International, 1971), 60.

10. Edward Michael Bankers Green, *I Believe in the Holy Spirit* (Grand Rapids, MI: William B. Eerdmans Publishing Company, 1975), 97.

11. Ernst Käsemann, *Commentary on Romans*, trans. Geoffrey Bromley (Grand Rapids, MI: William B. Eerdmans Publishing Company, 1980), 241.

12. H. Newton Malony, "Debunking Some of the Myths

about Glossolalia," in *Charismatic Experiences in History,* ed. Cecil M. Robeck, Jr. (Peabody, MA: Hendrickson Publishers, 1985), 102–110.

13. Harold Horton, *The Gifts of the Holy Spirit* (Nottingham, U.K.: The Assemblies of God Publishing House, 1968), 150.

14. See John F. MacArthur, Jr., *Charismatic Chaos* (Grand Rapids, MI: Zondervan Publishing House, 1992), 237–245.

15. Frank Stagg, *The Holy Spirit Today* (Nashville, TN: Broadman Press, 1973), 54.

16. A prime example was A. B. Simpson, whose policy in the Christian and Missionary Alliance churches was "Seek not, forbid not." See George H. Williams and Edith Waldvogel, "A History of Speaking in Tongues and Related Gifts," in *The Charismatic Movement,* ed. Michael P. Hamilton (Grand Rapids, MI: William B. Eerdmans Publishing Company, 1975), 100.

17. John Rea, *The Holy Spirit in the Bible: All the Major Passages about the Spirit—A Commentary* (Altamonte Springs, FL: Creation House, 1990), 267–268.

18. Howard Matthew Ervin, *This Which Ye See and Hear* (Plainfield, NJ: Logos International, 1972), 89.

19. Rea, *The Holy Spirit in the Bible,* 268.

20. Russell Spittler, "Gift of Interpretation of Tongues," in *Dictionary of Pentecostal and Charismatic Movements,* ed. Stanley M. Burgess, Gary B. McGee, and Patrick H. Alexander (Grand Rapids, MI: Zondervan Publishing House, 1988), 469.

21. Dennis Joseph Bennett and Rita Bennett, *The Holy Spirit and You: A Study Guide to the Spirit-Filled Life* (Plainfield, NJ: Logos International, 1971), 89.

22. Ibid. See also David Johannes du Plessis, *The Spirit Bade Me Go* (Plainfield, NJ: Logos International, 1977), 85.

Chapter 11

MOTIVATIONAL GIFTS

I MAGINE YOU ARE attending a seminar on worship. You have come to hear about the most recent approaches to entering God's presence. One pastor wants to learn how to get his congregation to worship through the singing of contemporary praise and worship choruses. Others are attending to investigate the latest worship technologies: overhead and rear screen projectors and other video reinforcement. Instead, the expert steps onto the stage and starts talking about becoming a living sacrifice.

"Who does he think we are?" some ask. The response of most is, "I just came here to find out how to transform my Sunday morning worship experience. This person wants to change how we live our whole lives."

BECOMING A LIVING SACRIFICE

Yet this is the message that the apostle Paul presented in his epistle to the church of Rome: *"Therefore, I urge you, brothers, in view of God's mercy, to offer your bodies as living sacrifices, holy and pleasing to God—this is your spiritual act of worship"* (Romans 12:1).

All the tools mentioned above are great. God employs new ways of doing things. We should explore using all of the wonderful technologies at our disposal. However, before anything else, the Lord requires one chief ingredient: He needs *all* of us. He must become Lord of our lives. Then He can use us effectively.

As in Corinth, and in almost any church, people compare themselves with others. Jealousy and envy plague the whole of humanity. A sense of perspective comes only when we recognize that God has called us to serve Him and that any abilities that we possess came from our Creator. These include both our natural talents and the enabling graces of the Holy Spirit. Sometimes, knowing where one stops and the other begins is difficult. Regardless, Paul made it clear that the Lord calls each of us to a unique mission. The Lord has placed motivations in our hearts that move us in the direction for which He has designed us. The apostle designated these motivational gifts as graces:

> *Just as each of us has one body with many members, and these members do not all have the same function, so in Christ we who are many form one body, and each member belongs to all the others. We have different gifts, according to the grace given us.*
>
> *(Romans 12:4–6)*

There was only one apostle Peter. There will never be another apostle Paul. There will only be one of you and one of me. God makes no carbon copies. Every one of us is an original!

The apostle Paul was not alone when he taught about motivational gifts. The apostle Peter, one of the closest associates of Jesus, wrote, *"Each one should use whatever gift he has received to serve others, faithfully administering God's grace in its various forms"* (1 Peter 4:10). For the Christian, the goals that drive us, our motivations, stem from God's favor. He places these motivations within us as the means to fulfill His purposes. In 1 Corinthians 12–14, Paul clarified that all believers and the gifts they receive are important. They are significant because they all work together to build up the church, the body of Christ. The gifts help us to serve one another better. Biblical scholar J. Ramsey Michaels asserts that in Romans 12, Paul

> accents the gifts of helping and serving even more than in 1 Corinthians 12, and makes no mention of tongues speaking, healing, or miracles....spiritual gifts are defined very broadly ...encompassing both the "natural" and the "supernatural."[1]

REFLECTIONS OF GOD'S NATURE

We have different gifts, according to the grace given us. If a man's gift is prophesying, let him use it in proportion to his faith. If it is serving, let him serve; if it is teaching, let him teach; if it is encouraging, let him encourage;

*if it is contributing to the needs of others, let
him give generously; if it is leadership, let him
govern diligently; if it is showing mercy, let
him do it cheerfully.*   *(Romans 12:6–8)*

Paul started this list of motivational gifts in
Romans 12 with inspired prophecy: *"If a man's gift
is prophesying, let him use it in proportion to his
faith"* (v. 6). First, he recognized that prophecy is a
gift. Next, he pointed out that it takes faith to bring
forth a prophecy. Consequently, Paul said that the
prophet is to speak *"in proportion to his faith."* To
speak prophetically, a person must be utterly convinced that he or she has a word from the Lord.
Vague and tentative descriptions lessen the impact
of the message being brought. With experience, a
person's faith grows. One is a prophet when one
functions as a prophet. Peter recommended that *"if
anyone speaks, he should do it as one speaking the
very words of God"* (1 Peter 4:11). We could apply
this instruction to teaching and preaching as well.

We must consider our words carefully when we
share things that are of the Lord. True Christian
prophets act in humility, submitting their words to
other recognized prophets and leaders in order to
discern whether those words constitute a communication from God. Having a grace to prophesy is different from wanting to control people as a prophet, a
problem we addressed in our study on prophecy. Any
motivation from God puts selfish ambition aside.

Regarding the one whose gift is serving, Paul
said that we should *"let him serve"* (Romans 12:7).

Remember, the word *minister* means "servant." Many people are impressed by those who are in the ministry, but all Christians are God's ministers, ordained to serve God. Some people stand out as having a servant's heart. They love to help people. They live to serve. This agrees with Peter's additional instructions: *"If anyone serves, he should do it with the strength God provides, so that in all things God may be praised through Jesus Christ"* (1 Peter 4:11).

There is another type of person, one who enjoys teaching others about God's Word and about how to live a godly life. Paul wrote concerning the person whose gift is teaching that the church should *"let him teach"* (Romans 12:7). The Greek word for teaching is *didasko*, which, in Greek culture, referred to the idea of extending the hand for acceptance, that is, causing one to accept something. The Hebrew notion of teaching focused on instruction in how to live rather than instruction in knowledge and skills. In the New Testament, the concept of teaching entailed furnishing believers with those things that God requires of the whole man, passing on truth to be preserved in the church, and calling people to follow Christ.[2]

Paul continued by saying that if a person's gift *"is encouraging, let him encourage"* (v. 8). Here Paul used the word *parakaleo*. Jesus used a related term, *paraclete*, to describe the Holy Spirit, a term that means the "counselor," the "one called alongside." In the Septuagint, the Greek translation of the Old Testament, *parakaleo* was used to translate the Hebrew concepts of comfort, having compassion, encouragement, strength, and being moved to pity.[3] In secular

Greek, the word meant "to call in assistance." Some translate this word "to exhort," that is, "to strongly urge." The word has the sense of both lifting people up when they are down and bringing them down when they have too high an opinion of themselves. People who are given this kind of motivation are great counselors.

Paul knew one encourager quite well—a man named Joseph. The believers began calling him Barnabas, which means "son of encouragement." For a period, Barnabas traveled with Paul. Then they parted ways due to a disagreement about a certain young man who ran off during a mission. Paul wanted nothing more to do with him. Barnabas, on the other hand, kept on encouraging this young man, John Mark. Barnabas restored Mark—the one on whom Paul had given up. This same Mark later wrote the Gospel that bears his name. Because of Barnabas's support, Mark was used to chronicle an important record of the life and ministry of Jesus. Encouragement, counseling, and exhortation are essential gifts to the church.

All of these motivational gifts are reflections of the nature of God. This is certainly true of the next gift Paul wrote about: *"If it is contributing to the needs of others, let him give generously"* (Romans 12:8). The word for "generous giving" is *metadidomi*, "to give a share in."[4] God gives certain people special abilities and grace to contribute to the needs of others.

However, it is important to remember that all Christians are called to give. God gives us blessings, and we are to bless others in turn. *"Freely you have received, freely give"* (Matthew 10:8). Paul instructed Timothy:

> *Command those who are rich in this present world not to be arrogant nor to put their hope in wealth, which is so uncertain, but to put their hope in God, who richly provides us with everything for our enjoyment. Command them to do good, to be rich in good deeds, and to be generous and willing to share. In this way they will lay up treasure for themselves as a firm foundation for the coming age, so that they may take hold of the life that is truly life.*
> *(1 Timothy 6:17–19)*

In Matthew 6:19–24, Jesus used several word pictures to illustrate how people are either generous or stingy. Those who have learned how to give have received this grace from our Creator. Through the years, my wife and I have had many opportunities to give to others. We have discovered that a person cannot outgive God. God has returned multiplied blessings to us through the years as we have given to the work of God.

Next, Paul wrote about the gift of leadership. An army cannot be made up entirely of generals. On the one hand, the church has one Commander in Chief, the Lord Jesus Christ. The Lord is our Shepherd (Psalm 23:1). On the other hand, God also raises up individuals to positions of leadership. Paul advised that if a person has the gift of leadership, *"let him govern diligently"* (Romans 12:8). The Greek word *prohisamenos*, meaning "the one at the head" or "the one taking the lead," represents the one who has gone on before and now knows how to show the way.[5] A leader is one who has learned to walk with God and obey His commands, being led by the Spirit. Such a leader is prepared to show people how to follow that same path. Paul counseled Timothy, *"If anyone sets his heart on being an overseer, he desires a noble task"* (1 Timothy 3:1).

Paul specified characteristics that are necessary for Christian leadership. A leader must be *"above reproach, the husband of but one wife"* (v. 2) and a responsible person of integrity. When the apostle wrote to the Roman church that a leader should *"govern diligently"* (Romans 12:8), he meant that leadership should represent "ethical action and behavior."[6] As a pastor and Christian leader, I have sought never to be lazy. God expects me to work for Him full-time, and that is something I have always tried to do. I show up at my office early. I write letters and make phone calls. I counsel and pray. I prepare my sermons. I visit the sick and elderly. I meet with other Christian leaders. I take my duties seriously. God expects us to do that. When we do, God's people are blessed and the work of the kingdom prospers.

Paul finished his list of motivational gifts by mentioning the one who has the gift of *"showing mercy"*; he said, *"Let him do it cheerfully"* (v. 8). The Greek word *eleon* connotes "having pity or compassion" on someone. For the Christian, it is never enough to feel sorry for others; a Christian searches for a way to do something about the problem as well. Paul spoke of himself as having received God's mercy and having been made trustworthy and an apostle. (See 1 Timothy 1:13, 16; 1 Corinthians 7:25.) Not to have mercy is to be ruthless. To be ruthless is one of the lowest things a person can become (Romans 1:28–31).[7] Once someone has received God's mercy, gratitude compels him to show compassion also. Therefore, Paul exhorted those who had been given the gift of showing mercy to give with cheerfulness. He used a form of the Greek word *hilaros*, meaning "cheerful or merry," from which we derive the word *hilarious*.

Christians should not minister to others out of a sense of duty alone but because they delight in being able to help someone. Giving is a joyful experience.[8] Jesus said, *"It is more blessed to give than to receive"* (Acts 20:35). Paul affirmed, *"God loves a cheerful giver"* (2 Corinthians 9:7). When we help one in need, we are actually ministering to Jesus. (See Matthew 25:34–40.)

We have received many blessings from God. Through His grace, the Lord has given us spiritual gifts. As we recognize these gifts, we must put them to use. When we do so, the Lord will be honored and His people will be blessed.

Notes

1. J. Ramsey Michaels, "Gifts of the Spirit," in *Charismatic Experiences in History,* ed. Cecil M. Robeck, Jr. (Peabody, MA: Hendrickson Publishers, 1985), 334.

2. Klaus Wegenast, "Teach," in *The New International Dictionary of New Testament Theology (NIDNTT),* ed. Colin Brown (Grand Rapids, MI: Zondervan Publishing House, 1978), 3:759–765.

3. Georg Braumann, "Exhort," *NIDNTT,* 1:569–571.

4. Hewart Vorländer, "Gift," *NIDNTT,* 2:40–43.

5. Lothar Coenan, "Bishop," *NIDNTT,* 1:188–201.

6. Wolfgang Bauder, "Zeal," *NIDNTT,* 3:1168–1169.

7. Hans-Helmut Esser, "Mercy," *NIDNTT,* 2:593–598.

8. Hans-Georg Link, "Reconciliation," *NIDNTT,* 3:148. See also Ernst Hoffmann, "Hope, Expectation," *NIDNTT,* 2:239.

Chapter 12

THE FRUIT OF THE SPIRIT

W E PLACE MUCH emphasis in our world today on the protection of our natural environment. As important as that is, shouldn't we in the church be paying even more attention to preserving the proper spiritual environment? Recognizing that God calls all believers to ministry is extremely significant. Being motivated by God to do what He has called us to do is essential. The supernatural manifestations of the Holy Spirit make us aware of God's presence and power in our midst. In addition, every gift, every grace, and every manifestation of God's Spirit should occur in an atmosphere of love.

For this reason, Paul put the Love Chapter (1 Corinthians 13) between a chapter on the diversity of gifts and a chapter on the operation of the gifts of prophesy, tongues, and interpretation. Remember, Jesus summarized the law of the old covenant with a single word: *love*. Love God, and love your neighbor!

Paul wrote, *"If I speak in the tongues of men and of angels, but have not love, I am only a resounding gong or a clanging cymbal"* (1 Corinthians 13:1).

Showing off our spiritual prowess while remaining unloving has an empty ring to it. Speaking in tongues is a wonderful gift from God, but unless we love others and please God, what good is it? We have missed the focal point of Christianity if we omit love.

"If I have the gift of prophecy and can fathom all mysteries and all knowledge, and if I have a faith that can move mountains, but have not love, I am nothing" (1 Corinthians 13:2). We might receive a word from the Lord. We might gain all kinds of spiritual insights. We might be able to believe God for anything. Yet if we neglect our family and forsake our friends, if we fail to forgive and show mercy to others, nothing will bring us satisfaction.

"If I give all I possess to the poor and surrender my body to the flames, but have not love, I gain nothing" (v. 3). While taking care of the poor is a part of the Gospel, if we do it in an unloving way, our purpose is defeated. God calls us to spread His love through both word and deed. What have we gained if we have sacrificed for God, even to the point of death, but have lived miserable, loveless lives? There is no reward in this. As John urged,

> *Dear friends, let us love one another, for love comes from God. Everyone who loves has been born of God and knows God. Whoever does not love does not know God, because God is love.*
> *(1 John 4:7–8)*

People invest in all kinds of things but forget to invest in heavenly treasures (Matthew 6:19–20). Jesus once said, *"What good will it be for a man if he gains the whole world, yet forfeits his soul?"* (Matthew 16:26). No one likes to lose on an investment. There is only one guaranteed investment; love always brings a good return. A person has everything to gain when he invests in love. *"Now these three remain: faith, hope and love. But the greatest of these is love"* (1 Corinthians 13:13).

THE GIFT OF CHRIST'S CHARACTER

Paul minced no words. People will reap what they sow:

> *Do not be deceived: God cannot be mocked. A man reaps what he sows. The one who sows to please his sinful nature, from that nature will reap destruction; the one who sows to please the Spirit, from the Spirit will reap eternal life.* *(Galatians 6:7–8)*

Paul challenges us as believers: *"Since we live by the Spirit, let us keep in step with the Spirit"* (5:25). If we are going to follow Jesus Christ, we should obey Him (John 14:15). What did Jesus teach? Love one another as He has loved us (15:12).

Jesus said we would know His followers by the fruit they produce (Matthew 7:16). In the natural world, fruit grows on a tree. Good fruit comes from good trees, and bad fruit comes from bad trees (v. 18). A tree does not try to grow fruit; a tree grows fruit naturally. An orange will not grow on an apple tree, neither will an apple grow on an orange tree.

As Paul said, if we are dominated by our flesh, that is, our selfish, sinful nature, we will reap corruption (Galatians 6:8). If we are controlled by the Spirit, this fact will be evident. There is a fruit of following God and a fruit of following one's sinful nature.

Galatians 5:19–21 lists the various fruits of the flesh:

> *Sexual immorality, impurity and debauchery; idolatry and witchcraft; hatred, discord, jealousy, fits of rage, selfish ambition, dissensions, factions and envy; drunkenness, orgies, and the like.*

Selfishness is at the heart of evil and gives birth to all sorts of hateful and immoral acts.

If you bear the wrong kind of fruit, you are the wrong kind of tree. Until you allow God to change what you are, you will not make it into God's kingdom (v. 21). Blessedly, when we genuinely repent, turn to God, and are born again, we do become different people. Paul depicted the spiritual harvest resulting from walking in the Spirit: *"But the fruit of the Spirit is love, joy, peace, patience, kindness, goodness, faithfulness, gentleness and self-control. Against such things there is no law"* (vv. 22–23).

The fruit of the Spirit is also a gift from God, a manifestation of the Holy Spirit. It is simply Christ's character being formed in us. Again, we find that love is the centerpiece. Notice that the passage uses the singular *"fruit"* as opposed to the plural "fruits" of the Holy Spirit. Paul constructed this passage to highlight a single spiritual grace: love. When the Holy Spirit controls our lives, He will produce love in us. Love results in generating the character of Christ in us.[1] The founder of Campus Crusade for Christ, Bill Bright, suggests understanding Paul's thought as follows:

> The fruit of the Spirit is love, and it is manifested in joy, peace, patience, kindness, goodness, faithfulness, gentleness and self-control: Joy is love's strength. Peace is love's security. Patience is love's endurance. Kindness is love's conduct. Goodness is love's character. Faithfulness is love's confidence. Gentleness is love's humility. Self-control is love's victory.[2]

There are different words for different kinds of love in the Greek language. There is *eros* (sexual love), *philia* (friendship love), and *storge* (family love). Finally, there is *agape*, a completely different kind of love. The first three types of love have reasons attached to them. Sexual love is based on physical attraction. Friendship love stems from common interests or circumstances. One has family love because of one's blood relationship to another and from living closely together. Agape, however, is the strong love that always wants the best for another and continues to love whatever the circumstances or whether or not that love is returned.[3]

Greek experts describe this Godlike love as "a generous move by one for the sake of the other."[4]

Agape love keeps on loving when other types of love would have stopped loving long before. This love is the love that God exhibited to humanity in sending His only Son to save us: *"For God so loved the world that he gave his one and only Son, that whoever believes in him shall not perish but have eternal life"* (John 3:16). This was the love Jesus displayed when He hung on the cross for my sins and yours. The Bible commands us to love God, our neighbors, and our brothers and sisters in Christ in this way.

While love is the primary fruit of the Spirit, we need to explore each aspect of it that is included in Paul's list in Galatians 5:22–23. First, true joy knows that God is in control and that we are in His care. Difficulties may come. Each day may not be full of laughs. We might not always be happy in the generally accepted sense of the word. Nevertheless, every single day can be full of joy. The word Paul used in this passage for joy, *chara*, is a joy outside ourselves, because it is the "joy of faith."[5] It is the *"joy of the LORD,"* which Scripture tells us is our *"strength"* (Nehemiah 8:10).

Peace is not necessarily the absence of conflict but the sense of harmony we have when we are synchronized with God's will. When we are in line with God's will, everything is in order. Peace overcomes anxiety and fear, and it gives rest. The source of peace is the Lord alone. *Shalom,* a Hebrew word meaning "peace," has frequently been used as a greeting by the Jewish people. In John's gospel, we read that Jesus gives a type of peace to His followers that the world never could—the peace of God (John

14:27). The apostle Paul often opened his letters with a greeting of "grace and peace." For peace he used the word *eirene,* the same word he used in the list of the fruit of the Spirit.

The Greek word translated "patience," *makrothymia,* literally means the prolonged restraint of anger (*thymos*). Some translate *makrothymia* as "long-suffering." It is an ability that God gives us so that we may meet our neighbors halfway and share our lives with them. God's way is for us to put up with things we do not want to put up with, even when we are not forced to do so.[6]

The next thing Paul mentioned is kindness. The Greek word *chrestotes* describes a thoughtfulness that Christians should display toward someone; it can also be seen as friendliness. This means Christians do nice things for people although they do not have to.[7]

After kindness comes goodness, a similar concept. The Greek word *agathosyne,* meaning "goodness, uprightness, or generosity," comes from the root word *agathos,* meaning "that which is generally good and useful." It especially refers to moral goodness.[8]

A Christian is also somebody characterized by faithfulness, that is, one who is "full of faith." Earlier in this study, we surveyed the word *pistis.* This word can mean both "faith" and "faithfulness." We should keep in mind that biblical faith concerns putting our total trust in God. One who is full of faith will stand firm, whatever the circumstances, and will not easily be shaken.[9]

The word *gentleness, praytes* in Greek, has the sense of meekness and humility. It is "to be benevolent, the opposite of being harsh and brutal." It has an element of being considerate. It is the concrete expression of Christian love.[10]

The word translated as "self-control" is *egkrateia*. This word is a combination of two Greek words, meaning "self" and "strength." It means "to be able to take possession of oneself, to rule oneself, to take hold or grasp oneself."[11] Christians are not controlled by the whims of other forces. They are not out of control, in an ecstatic state, or undisciplined. Christian believers are not enslaved by anything or anyone but God.

Paul ended this section by saying that not one thing in his list violates the law of God (Galatians 5:23). Earlier, the apostle wrote, *"The entire law is summed up in a single command: 'Love your neighbor as yourself'"* (v. 14).[12] The old covenant listed a series of thou-shalt-nots. In the Christian life, believers fulfill the law naturally. As the ancient prophet foresaw in regard to the Messiah's new covenant, the Spirit of God has written God's law in the minds and on the hearts of Christians (Jeremiah 31:33).

John wrote that we are able to love because God first loved us (1 John 4:19). Love is a gift from God as well as the fruit of the Spirit. It summarizes the character of Christ and is the lubricant that makes all things run smoothly. While love is not the totality of God, certainly *"God is love"* (1 John 4:16)! I appeal to you with the words of Christ: *"My command is this: Love each other as I have loved you. Greater love has no one than this, that he lay down his life for his friends"* (John 15:12–13).

Notes

1. William Bright, *The Holy Spirit: The Key to Supernatural Living* (San Bernardino, CA: New Life Publications, 1980), 163.

2. Ibid., 164.

3. For a fuller discussion of the various Greek words for love and their Hebrew equivalents, see Walther Günther and Hans-Georg Link, "Love," in *The New International Dictionary of New Testament Theology (NIDNTT)*, ed. Colin Brown (Grand Rapids, MI: Zondervan Publishing House, 1978), 2:538–547.

4. Ibid., 539.

5. Erich Beyreuther and Günter Finkenrath, "Joy," *NIDNTT*, 2:359.

6. Ulrich Falkenroth and Colin Brown, "Patience," *NIDNTT*, 2:768–772.

7. Erich Beyreuther, "Good," *NIDNTT*, 2:105.

8. Ibid., 98–102.

9. Otto Michel, "Faith," *NIDNTT*, 1:599–606.

10. Wolfgang Bauder, "Humility," *NIDNTT*, 2:256–259.

11. Georg Braumann, "Strength," *NIDNTT*, 3:716–718.

12. Jesus' statements in the Gospels summarizing the law are found in Matthew 22:37–40; Mark 12:30–31; Luke 10:25–28; and John 15:10–12.

Chapter 13

THE GIFTS OF PRAYER AND FASTING

ONE OF THE most precious gifts God gives His people is the privilege to communicate directly with Him. We have seen how praying in tongues is a spiritual gift; praying with our understanding should also be directed by the Spirit. To be entitled to pray is indeed a gift of God.

CONVERSATION WITH GOD

Prayer is simply talking with God. It is not only talking to God but also listening in order to hear from God. We pray together publicly when we gather as Christian congregations. Prayer is also to take place in secret, in our own prayer closets.

Prayer can be a great time of spiritual refreshing, although at times it can also be extremely physically tiring. It is the great link with God that develops our relationships with Him and permits us to be used more efficiently in His service. There is no designated place where we have to pray. As I previously mentioned, we do not have to pray in a fancy room, just wherever we can go to be alone with God. We can pray in a cathedral or in an alley. We can pray on a hill or by the seashore. Jesus said that the place does not matter; what counts is our mode of prayer. When we worship our Father, we must come *"in spirit and in truth"* (John 4:24). This indicates that we must be guided by the Spirit; we must put aside all of our own pretensions. Because Jesus paid for our sins on the cross, we can boldly approach the throne of God (Hebrews 4:16).

There are many different positions we can take when we pray. We can certainly bow our heads, close our eyes, and bend our knees. We can also raise our eyes toward heaven. We can prostrate ourselves on the floor, or we can converse with God as we take walks. Some prefer to stand with their hands and heads raised toward heaven. Drawings of early Christian believers show them looking straight ahead, eyes open, with their hands raised. The positions of our bodies are not important; the positions of our hearts are what count.[1]

How do we pray? This is a question Jesus' own disciples asked Him. As we contemplate the model prayer Jesus gave His followers, which is found in Matthew 6, we see that we start by acknowledging our relationship to God. We begin with, *"Our Father"* (v. 9). Think about the implications of that: we may call the Creator of the heavens and earth our Father. He is *"our Father in heaven"* (v. 9).

Then we move into praise and worship. God alone is worthy of our adoration. We pray,

The Gifts of Prayer and Fasting

"Hallowed be your name" (Matthew 6:9). Whenever we pray, we should always spend time loving our God before we start asking petitions of Him.

Next, we are to seek His will in our lives. We pray, *"Your kingdom come, your will be done on earth as it is in heaven"* (v. 10). There has been extensive discussion among Christians about God's kingdom. The word in the Greek connotes "God's rule, reign, or government." His kingdom initially entered our world at the first coming of Jesus (Matthew 4:17); it will be consummated at His second coming. Meanwhile, we are to pray for God's reign to be established, first in our lives and then in the lives of those around us.

God is concerned about our needs. We are to pray about everything and not be anxious about anything (Philippians 4:6). So we pray, *"Give us today our daily bread"* (Matthew 6:11). Notice that we are to ask for today's provision, not tomorrow's or next month's. We are supposed to rely on Him to provide for us each and every day. The psalmist claimed he had never seen God forsake the righteous or their children (Psalm 37:25). Paul confirmed that, as believers, we can depend on God to provide for all of our needs (Philippians 4:19).

In prayer, we are always obliged to deal with the matter of sin. Sin tarnishes our relationships with God and with our neighbors. Consequently, we pray, *"Forgive us our debts, as we also have forgiven our debtors"* (Matthew 6:12). If we are to be forgiven, we must also forgive. Unforgiveness is a horrible bondage and may keep God from answering our prayers (Mark 11:25–26 KJV).

We are to ask Him, *"Lead us not into temptation"* (Matthew 6:13). Only a fool wants to be tempted. The Devil is all around us; he is like a roaring lion, waiting to see whom he can destroy (1 Peter 5:8). Fortunately, Christians can trust God to *"deliver us from the evil one"* (Matthew 6:13).

Paul asserted that we need to *"pray continually"* (1 Thessalonians 5:17; see also Ephesians 6:18). We should get away by ourselves in solitude and pray as the Spirit leads, taking time to grow in our relationships with God and to *"remain in the vine"* (John 15:4), our Lord Jesus.

TRUE FASTING PLEASES GOD

Now, what about fasting? Jesus fasted for forty days as He commenced His ministry (Matthew 4:1–11). The early church fasted and prayed (Acts 13:2; 14:23). Jesus taught that there are times to fast and there are times to feast (Mark 2:18–20). Paul spoke of times of prayer in which people may even refrain from marital relations (1 Corinthians 7:5). Old Testament saints often included fasting as a part of times of serious prayer (Joel 1:14). The prophet Isaiah instructed us to make sure our attitudes are right when we fast (Isaiah 58:1–12). Simply abstaining from food does little good. Not only are we to spend time in prayer with God, but we are also to ensure that we are living our lives in a just manner. We are to help the poor and oppressed. When we fast, we should take the money we are saving on food and share it with the hungry.[2] This type of fasting pleases God.

Fasting often accompanied prayer in the Bible. I have personally found it to be a powerful tool in my walk with God. Through it, I have received tremendous breakthroughs in being used as an instrument of God's Spirit.

THE IMPORTANCE OF PRAYER AND FASTING

Some time ago, the Holy Spirit directed me to go on an extended fast. I fasted for forty days and nights without drinking juice, eating food, or taking vitamins; I drank only water. During the process, extraordinary miracles happened in my life. The Holy Spirit brought demon-possessed people to me, and they received their deliverance. God delivered numerous people as I spoke with them over the telephone. Individuals called from various states and said, "I need deliverance," "I am demon-possessed," "I am bound by the power of the Devil," and, every time, God delivered them and set them free.

On the fortieth day, the final day of my fast, I was scheduled to preach in the city auditorium in Knoxville, Tennessee. All the full-gospel churches in the Knoxville area were sponsoring the meeting. The auditorium was jam-packed with people eager to receive their miracles of deliverance. Because of the fast, I had lost an incredible amount of weight. I remained behind the curtain on the platform until I was presented to minister. The pastor who introduced me said, "Ladies and gentlemen, don't be shocked when Brother Lowery comes to minister. He is not sick. He has just concluded a forty-day fast."

When I walked onto the platform, I could hear sounds all over the building as people caught their breaths because I was so thin. One pastor helped me walk to the podium, and I rested my weight on a tall stool as I ministered to the people. The audio technician turned up the volume of the microphones extremely high so that as I talked in a very low tone of voice, I could still be heard. As I talked, the Spirit of God gripped the audience. God's glory was so thick that it seemed as if you could have cut it with a knife.

After I had finished ministering the Word, I gave an invitation to all who wanted to be saved. Hundreds stood to receive Christ as their Savior. We prayed the sinner's prayer together, and a tremendous emotional outburst of praise filled the place as men and women received Christ. Then I asked those who desired to be filled with the Holy Spirit to stand. Hundreds stood; as we prayed, they were baptized with the Holy Spirit and began to speak with other tongues *as the Spirit gave them utterance* (Acts 2:4 KJV).

Next, I felt led to minister to the sick. I asked everyone in the audience who needed a miracle to stand and lay their hands on their bodies where the pain or the afflictions were, and to believe God for their miracles. There was such intense faith in the service that everyone expected to receive their miracles. As I prayed very quietly, God's healing power swept through the congregation. I believe God healed every person there. People leaped out of wheelchairs and off their cots, rejoicing and dancing in the Spirit. People with goiters experienced an immediate deliverance as the swelling vanished. Blind eyes were opened. Deaf ears were unstopped. Diabetes and heart conditions were cured. God healed all manner of sickness and disease that night by the mighty move of His Spirit.

God allowed us to enter into a dimension of supernatural glory in which He was pleased to pour out His Spirit upon the people in an extraordinary way.

THE ADVENTURE CONTINUES

The life of a Christian is exciting. Understanding the full Gospel means coming to realize that Christianity is so much more than joining a church and asking God for forgiveness. Christian discipleship is a lifestyle energized by God's presence. The Lord is with us and lives His life through us.

No Christian can be expected to live a life that is pleasing to God, in his or her own strength. Yet as he or she surrenders to God, such a life will not only be possible, but it will also be inevitable. The fullness of the Christian life is certainly an adventure, one that did not end with the book of Acts but continues in the life of every Christian believer today.

In our study of the Scriptures, along with the evidence of our experiences, we find that the Christian life is a life of grace. We are beneficiaries of the

Lord's favor, a favor that is unmerited and yet so needed. God gives us gifts to enable us to extend His love to others so that they too will find a relationship with Him. God has poured out His Spirit upon His church so that we may manifest His presence among the people of this world in this age. For us, as believers in the risen Jesus, it is a foretaste of what we will experience in eternity.

As a result of recent moves of the Holy Spirit, we see God's people mobilizing across denominational and cultural boundaries. We are one in God's Spirit, and we are one in Jesus Christ, our Savior and Lord (1 Corinthians 12:12–13).

I pray that this study of God's precious gifts will enable you to live a full and meaningful life, directed by God's Spirit and strengthened by His grace. Jesus told us that we are to be about His work until He returns (Luke 19:13). Reviewing our findings, we know how to accomplish this. First, we must ensure that we are truly born again. Then we must be empowered by His Spirit. As God's motivational gifts influence us and as we are open to the manifestations of the Holy Spirit, the Lord will develop our ministries. God has called us and will complete the work in us, as we obey Him (Philippians 1:6).

We are a colony of heaven (Philippians 3:20) and ambassadors of Christ (2 Corinthians 5:20). It is my prayer that all of us will faithfully submit to the rule of our King and permit Him to live His life through us, in the power of the marvelous Holy Spirit. May we keep on being filled with His Spirit, as we await the joyful coming of Jesus.

Notes

1. For an excellent short and easy-to-read book on prayer, see Chuck Smith, *Effective Prayer Life* (Costa Mesa, CA: Maranatha House Publisher, 1979).

2. For a wonderful book on fasting, see Arthur Wallis, *God's Chosen Fast* (Fort Washington, PA: Christian Literature Crusade, 1968).

References

‡Alexander, Patrick H. "Slain in the Spirit." In *Dictionary of Pentecostal and Charismatic Movements*.

†Bauder, Wolfgang. "Humility." In *The New International Dictionary of New Testament Theology*. Vol. 2.

†———. "Zeal." In *The New International Dictionary of New Testament Theology*. Vol. 3.

Bennett, Dennis Joseph. *Nine O'Clock in the Morning*. Plainfield, NJ: Logos International, 1970.

Bennett, Dennis Joseph and Rita Bennett. *The Holy Spirit and You: A Study Guide to the Spirit-Filled Life*. Plainfield, NJ: Logos International, 1971.

†Beyreuther, Erich. "Good." In *The New International Dictionary of New Testament Theology*. Vol. 2.

†Beyreuther, Erich and Günter Finkenrath. "Joy." In *The New International Dictionary of New Testament Theology*. Vol. 2.

†Braumann, Georg. "Exhort." In *The New International Dictionary of New Testament Theology*. Vol. 1.

†———. "Strength." In *The New International Dictionary of New Testament Theology*. Vol. 3.

Bredesen, Harald and Pat King. *Yes, Lord*. Plainfield, NJ: Logos International, 1972.

Bright, William. *The Holy Spirit: The Key to Super-natural Living*. San Bernardino, CA: New Life Publications, 1980.

Brown, Colin. *Miracles and the Critical Mind*. Grand Rapids, MI: William B. Eerdmans Publishing Company, 1984.

†——. "Proclamation, Preach, Kerygma." In *The New International Dictionary of New Testament Theology*. Vol. 3.

†——. "Prophet." In *The New International Dictionary of New Testament Theology*. Vol. 3.

Bruner, Frederick Dale. *A Theology of the Holy Spirit: The Pentecostal Experience and the New Testament Witness*. Grand Rapids, MI: William B. Eerdmans Publishing Company, 1970.

‡Burgess, Stanley M. "Doctrine of the Holy Spirit: The Ancient Fathers." In *Dictionary of Pentecostal and Charismatic Movements*.

Christenson, Larry. *Speaking in Tongues and Its Significance for the Church*. Minneapolis, MN: Dimension Books, 1968.

†Coenan, Lothar. "Bishop." In *The New International Dictionary of New Testament Theology*. Vol. 1.

Cross, Frank Leslie and Elizabeth Anne Livingstone, eds. *The Oxford Dictionary of the Christian Church*. Oxford: Oxford University Press, 1974.

Dunn, James Douglas Grant. *Baptism in the Holy Spirit: A Re-Examination of the New Testament Teaching on the Gift of the Spirit in Relation to Pentecostalism Today*. Philadelphia: The Westminster Press, 1970.

———. *Jesus and the Spirit: A Study of the Religious and Charismatic Experience of Jesus and the First Christians as Reflected in the New Testament.* Philadelphia: The Westminster Press, 1975.

Du Plessis, David Johannes. "Holy Spirit in Ecumenical Movement." In *Jesus, Where Are You Taking Us?: Messages from the First International Lutheran Conference on the Holy Spirit.* Edited by Norris Wogen. Carol Stream, IL: Creation House, 1973.

———. *The Spirit Bade Me Go.* Plainfield, NJ: Logos International, 1977.

Du Plessis, David Johannes and Bob Slosser. *A Man Called Mr. Pentecost.* Plainfield, NJ: Logos International, 1977.

Ervin, Howard Matthew. *And Forbid Not to Speak with Tongues.* Plainfield, NJ: Logos International, 1971.

———. *Conversion-Initiation and the Baptism in the Holy Spirit.* Peabody, MA: Hendrickson Publishers, 1987.

———. *Spirit Baptism: A Biblical Investigation.* Peabody, MA: Hendrickson Publishers, 1987.

———. *This Which Ye See and Hear.* Plainfield, NJ: Logos International, 1972.

†Esser, Hans-Helmut. "Mercy." In *The New International Dictionary of New Testament Theology.* Vol. 2.

†Falkenroth, Ulrich and Colin Brown. "Patience." In *The New International Dictionary of New Testament Theology.* Vol. 2.

Finney, Charles Grandison. *Power from on High*. Ft. Washington, PA: Christian Literature Crusade, 1949.

§Ford, Josephine Massyngberde. "The Charismatic Gifts in Worship." In *The Charismatic Movement*.

*Gelpi, Donald L., S. J. "Breath-Baptism in the Synoptics." In *Charismatic Experiences in History*.

George, Bill. *Added to the Church: A Church of God Membership Manual*. Cleveland, TN: Pathway Press, 1987.

Gillquist, Peter E. *Let's Quit Fighting about the Holy Spirit*. Grand Rapids, MI: Zondervan Publishing House, 1974.

†Goetzman, J. "Wisdom: Sophia." In *The New International Dictionary of New Testament Theology*. Vol. 3.

Green, Edward Michael Bankers. *I Believe in the Holy Spirit*. Grand Rapids, MI: William B. Eerdmans Publishing Company, 1975.

———. *Who Is This Jesus?* Nashville, TN: Thomas Nelson Publishers, 1992.

†Günther, Walther, Hans-Georg Link, and Colin Brown. "Love." In *The New International Dictionary of New Testament Theology*. Vol. 2.

Hanegraff, Hank. *Christianity in Crisis*. Eugene, OR: Harvest House Publishers, 1993.

Harper, Michael. *Let My People Grow: Ministry and Leadership in the Church*. Plainfield, NJ: Logos International, 1977.

References

†Hoffman, Ernst. "Hope, Expectation." In *The New International Dictionary of New Testament Theology*. Vol. 2.

Hollenweger, Walter J. *The Pentecostals*. Minneapolis, MN: Augsburg Publishing House, 1972.

Horton, Harold. *The Gifts of the Holy Spirit*. Nottingham, U.K.: The Assemblies of God Publishing House, 1968.

Hummel, Charles G. *Fire in the Fireplace: Contemporary Charismatic Renewal*. Downers Grove, IL: InterVarsity Press, 1978.

Käsemann, Ernst. *Commentary on Romans*. Translated by Geoffrey Bromley. Grand Rapids, MI: William B. Eerdmans Publishing Company, 1980.

Kraft, Charles H. *Christianity with Power: Your Worldview and Your Experience of the Supernatural*. Ann Arbor, MI: Vine Books, 1989.

Küng, Hans. *Does God Exist?: An Answer for Today*. Translated by Edward Quinn. Garden City, NY: Doubleday, 1980.

Ladd, George Eldon. *The Presence of the Future*. Grand Rapids, MI: William B. Eerdmans Publishing Company, 1974.

Lightfoot, J. B. and J. R. Harmer, eds. *The Apostolic Fathers*. Grand Rapids, MI: Baker Book House, 1956.

†Link, Hans-Georg. "Reconciliation." In *The New International Dictionary of New Testament Theology*. Vol. 3.

MacArthur, John F., Jr. *Charismatic Chaos*. Grand Rapids, MI: Zondervan Publishing House, 1992.

MacNutt, Francis. *Healing.* 2d ed. New York: Doubleday, 1990.

——. *Overcome by the Spirit.* Old Tappan, NJ: Chosen Books, 1990.

——. *The Power to Heal.* Notre Dame, IN: Ave Maria Press, 1977.

*Malony, H. Newton. "Debunking Some of the Myths about Glossolalia." In *Charismatic Experiences in History.*

Martin, George. *Healing: Reflections on the Gospel.* Ann Arbor, MI: Servant Books, 1977.

McDonnell, Kilian, ed. *The Holy Spirit and Power: The Catholic Charismatic Renewal.* Garden City, NY: Doubleday, 1975.

*Michaels, J. Ramsey. "Gifts of the Spirit." In *Charismatic Experiences in History.*

†Michel, Otto. "Faith." In *The New International Dictionary of New Testament Theology.* Vol. 1.

Moule, Charles Francis Digby. *The Holy Spirit.* Grand Rapids, MI: William B. Eerdmans Publishing Company, 1978.

Mühlen, Heribert. *A Charismatic Theology: Initiation in the Spirit.* New York: Paulist Press, 1978.

Osborn, Tommy Lee. *Healing the Sick.* Tulsa, OK: Osborne Foundation, 1959.

Pamphilus, Eusebius. *Ecclesiastical History.* Translated by Christian Frederick Cruse. Grand Rapids, MI: Baker Book House, 1977.

Pinnock, Clark H. and Robert C. Brow. *Unbounded Love: A Good News Theology for the Twenty-First*

Century. Downers Grove, IL: InterVarsity Press, 1994.

Ramsey, Michael. *Holy Spirit*. Grand Rapids, MI: William B. Eerdmans Publishing Company, 1977.

Rea, John. *The Holy Spirit in the Bible: All the Major Passages about the Spirit—A Commentary*. Altamonte Springs, FL: Creation House, 1990.

*Robeck, Cecil M., Jr. "Origen's Treatment of the Charismata in 1 Corinthians 12:8–10." In *Charismatic Experiences in History*.

‡———. "Word of Wisdom." In *Dictionary of Pentecostal and Charismatic Movements*.

Runia, Klaas. "The Trinity." In *Nelson's Introduction to the Christian Faith*. Edited by Robin Keeley. Nashville, TN: Thomas Nelson Publishers, 1992.

Scanlon, Michael and Anne Therese Shields. *And Their Eyes Were Opened: Encountering Jesus in the Sacraments*. Notre Dame, IN: The Word of Life, 1976.

†Schmitz, E. D. "Knowledge: Ginosko." In *The New International Dictionary of New Testament Theology*. Vol. 2.

Shakarian, Demos, John L. Sherrill, and Elizabeth Sherrill. *The Happiest People on Earth*. Lincoln, VA: Chosen Books, 1975.

Sherrill, John L. *They Speak with Other Tongues*. Old Tappan, NJ: Spire Books, 1964.

Smith, Chuck. *Effective Prayer Life*. Costa Mesa, CA: Maranatha House Publisher, 1979.

‡Spittler, Russell. "Gift of Interpretation of Tongues." In *Dictionary of Pentecostal and Charismatic Movements.*

‡——. "Glossolalia." In *Dictionary of Pentecostal and Charismatic Movements.*

Stagg, Frank. *The Holy Spirit Today.* Nashville, TN: Broadman Press, 1973.

Stiles, J. E. *The Gift of the Holy Spirit.* Glendale, CA: The Church Press, n.d.

Stott, John R. W. *Baptism and Fullness: The Work of the Holy Spirit Today.* 2d ed. Downers Grove, IL: InterVarsity Press, 1976.

Stronstad, Roger. *The Charismatic Theology of St. Luke.* Peabody, MA: Hendrickson Publishers, 1984.

Suenens, Leon-Joseph Cardinal. *A New Pentecost?* New York: Seabury Press, 1974.

Synan, Vinson. *In the Latter Days: The Outpouring of the Holy Spirit in the Twentieth Century.* 2d ed. Ann Arbor, MI: Servant Publications, 1991.

——. *The Twentieth Century Pentecostal Explosion: The Exciting Growth of Pentecostal Churches and Charismatic Renewal Movements.* Altamonte Springs, FL: Creation House, 1987.

Taylor, Jack R. *After the Spirit Comes.* Nashville, TN: Broadman Press, 1974.

——. *The Word of God with Power.* Nashville, TN: Broadman and Holdman, Publishers, 1993.

Torrey, Reuben Archer. *The Baptism with the Holy Spirit.* Minneapolis, MN: Dimension Books, 1972.

References

Underwood, B. E. *The Gifts of the Spirit: Supernatural Equipment for Christian Service.* Franklin Springs, GA: Advocate Press, 1967.

——. *Spiritual Gifts: Ministries and Manifestations.* Franklin Springs, GA: Advocate Press, 1984.

†Vorländer, Hewart. "Gift." In *The New International Dictionary of New Testament Theology.* Vol. 2.

Wagner, Charles Peter. *The Third Wave of the Holy Spirit.* Ann Arbor, MI: Vine Books, 1988.

——. *Your Spiritual Gifts Can Help Your Church Grow: How to Find Your Gift and Use It.* Glendale, CA: Gospel Light Regal Books, 1979.

Wallis, Arthur. *God's Chosen Fast.* Fort Washington, PA: Christian Literature Crusade, 1968.

——. *Pray in the Spirit: The Work of the Holy Spirit in the Ministry of Prayer.* Fort Washington, PA: Christian Literature Crusade, 1970.

Watson, David. *I Believe in the Church.* Grand Rapids, MI: William B. Eerdmans Publishing Company, 1978.

†Wegenast, Klaus. "Teach." In *The New International Dictionary of New Testament Theology.* Vol. 3.

§Williams, George H. and Edith Waldvogel. "A History of Speaking in Tongues and Related Gifts." In *The Charismatic Movement.*

Williams, John Rodman. *The Gift of the Holy Spirit Today: The Greatest Reality of the Twentieth Century.* Plainfield, NJ: Logos International, 1980.

——. *The Pentecostal Reality*. Plainfield, NJ: Logos International, 1972.

Wimber, John and Kevin Springer. *Power Healing*. New York: Harper and Row, 1987.

† *The New International Dictionary of New Testament Theology*. 3 vols. Edited by Colin Brown. Grand Rapids, MI: Zondervan Publishing House, 1978.

‡ *Dictionary of Pentecostal and Charismatic Movements*. Edited by Stanley M. Burgess, Gary B. McGee, and Patrick H. Alexander. Grand Rapids, MI: Zondervan Publishing House, 1988.

§ *The Charismatic Movement*. Edited by Michael P. Hamilton. Grand Rapids, MI: William B. Eerdmans Publishing Company, 1975.

* *Charismatic Experiences in History*. Edited by Cecil M. Robeck, Jr. Peabody, MA: Hendrickson Publishers, 1985.